I0438087

THE FIRST BLACK NATION

Relentless Quest

Vladimir Guerrier

authorHOUSE®

AuthorHouse™
1663 Liberty Drive
Bloomington, IN 47403
www.authorhouse.com
Phone: 1-800-839-8640

© 2009 Vladimir Guerrier. All rights reserved.

No part of this book may be reproduced, stored in a retrieval system, or transmitted by any means without the written permission of the author.

First published by AuthorHouse 5/21/2009

ISBN: 978-1-4389-7064-6 (e)
ISBN: 978-1-4389-7063-9 (sc)

Printed in the United States of America
Bloomington, Indiana

This book is printed on acid-free paper.

ONE QUESTION MANY ANSWERS

There is a beginning to everything in existence, a genuine source, from which answers to all questions could be found.

During the course of my life, I have found myself seeking for answers to many questions my mind has conceived over the years, and I always have to prioritize their relevance, their value, their importance in relations with my life, my environment, and the society in which I live. Some of those questions are trivial and irrelevant to my personal life, but they do have great significance to life in general. Some of them remain mysteries that I believe no man alive could ever satisfy me with answers for. Some are so vast in definition and explanation; everyone could come up with so many different answers for them, to the point of creating controversies among a whole civilization.

I was frequently reprimanded by one of my girlfriends for asking too many questions, especially when we spoke over the phone, for I'm not a talkative person when it comes to phone conversation, I usually tend to get sidetracked easily by other activities around me, that I sometime subconsciously blocked her out of my head. She always thought I was being nosy or curious, or I was purposely getting on her nerves. Nevertheless, I recall my defensive response had always been the same; I would tell her that a conversation is mainly based on questions and answers, and without them, a real conversation could be hardly developed. But the truth of the matter is, sometimes I just didn't know what to say, and I always hoped a question would get the ball rolling toward an interesting conversation, which was not always the case.

Knowledge begins with questions, questions lead to research, and out of research come answers. But sometimes a question may have various answers in contrast to one source and others, depending on what different people think the answer should be, or prominent philosophers and thorough researchers believe the answer to be. Therefore which answer is correct to a particular question, is another question to be puzzling about.

I have witnessed brothers and sisters getting frustrated by their younger siblings, because young children never seem to run out of questions. But even when those inquiries from a toddler may seem to be of no value or interest to a grown up, they may have profound effects which may impact a child throughout a lifetime. That is the reason why parents should be vigilant on what they say and do around their children; who their children are being taught by, and what type of environment their children are being exposed to. Children are true imitators, who are intelligent at capturing and retaining physical, visual and audible data. On a different level of course, a grown person as well should be vigilant when it comes to seeking for answers to whatever an interest or curiosity may be, while the main source is not always easy to spot. A man would only tell people what he wants them to know, and he would try vehemently to make people believe what he wants them to believe, simply for his vicious gain and his personal exploit.

THE SOURCE

I'm not trying to convince anyone that this book is the source of truth, because I too, from my own judgment had to choose sources upon which some of my statements and supports are based, and hope they are reliable enough and truthful. But I urge all readers to be at ease, for everything mentioned in this book is either physically or topographically proven to be accurate, even what historians have previously published, have been re-evaluated for better and satisfactory results. Some of the topics in this book are also based on revelations from a higher dimension; some are based on my personal experiences, understanding, and perceptions of life and cosmogony. I don't expect everyone to agree with me on anything written therein unless otherwise a common view or interest is felt; I am only one man with my own opinion on a category of things. However, the most significant factors written in this publication such as the origin of man, the distinction of races, and anything with a religious aspect, are from my personal exegesis from the main Source; The Bible.

DISCRIMINATION AND
RACISM MEAN HATRED

As a black man, I have heard of so many discriminatory incidents and injustice that people of my complexion have suffered in the past, subtly even today in our communities, and I feel helpless that I'm not in the position to give solace to victims of those hateful treatments. Even to this day the effects never dissipate, they linger with me, ravaging my soul, and then I would find myself wondering about certain factors. I have watched documentaries, I have heard from the news over the radio, and on television, I have read from books, magazines and newspapers, about black people being battered, murdered and mistreated, even in the most famous establishments, just for being who they are. Because they carry a skin color that is naturally and biologically possessed, a condition that is out of anyone's control. They didn't choose to have the hair texture that they carry, nor did they have any say in acquiring those thick kissable lips that some of them have. But they were blessed to be formed by the Creator the way they are. Racism and discrimination are unjustifiable and intolerable.

Out of all those confusions, I began to come up with some questions of my own, and I was compelled and determined to do research about my past, about my origin, so I can balance the primitive era with where we am today, in the efforts to find some comprehension, and try to make some sense out certain events, and other people's perceptions on various factors and reactions to certain actions. I concluded to realize that we have not made great progress from the hatred that was shown toward us in the fourteenth century, down the line to the present. Racism is much alive today, discrimination is still a common practice almost everywhere we go, and hatred has pervaded our world. It is simply suppressed and latent in some places. Like a volcano that has been dormant for years and may one day erupt unexpectedly, although the villagers know it's there, but because they don't know when it's going to erupt, and because no one can prevent it from happening, they can only be educated on how to be prepared, on what they should do and how to approach the situation when it actually happens, and so is the case when it comes to racism and discrimination, which to me are summed up to be hatred altogether.

Writing about discrimination and racism and hatred, I have no choice but to express myself on how I feel about slavery, which is an important part of the nation this book is all about.

The purpose of this book is to propagandize the history of a great people, to let everyone know who the First Black Nation in the world is, how that title was claimed, and how they consequently became the first Republic in the Western Hemisphere.

I want to start with the young Haitians of this generation, going forward to generations to come, for them to know about their history, but I also want every nation on earth to know about the Haitian people, and their unparallel histories which have been neglected and ignored for centuries. I want every black child, every black man and woman to be educated on who they are, where they are from, and how their histories came about, because the histories of racism and slavery concern particularly everyone who is a descendant of the African continent. It would be an incomplete work, or should I go as far to say impossible to write about how a people came out of slavery, and how they have earned such an irreversible title as the First Black Nation in the world, and not talk about the Motherland, out of which not only dark skinned people are from but where mankind wholly originated. Whether anyone believes it or not, it is true and there's nothing anyone can do about it but to deny it, which would in turn be denial of one's originality.

What does the word race mean? The definition of that word in any dictionary is found to have two distinctive meanings. One definition for the word race, is to compete with others at a level of speed to reach a destination or complete a task first. The other definition is, any of several subdivisions of mankind sharing certain physical characteristics, especially color of skin, color and type of hair, and shape of eyes and nose. It's incredible to hear that there are men and women who actually make it a career to study people living on this planet, and categorize them by types and qualities. How frivolous? They propagated that there are three types of people in the world according to races: the Negroid, the Caucasoid, and the Mongoloid. Unlike the philosophies of some, race to me is not defined by physical characteristics, or the color of someone's skin, or the color and type of hair of a person, but by the form and attributes of living creatures like the reptiles, the birds, the mammals, the rodents and the insects. There is only one race in which a man or a woman can be categorized regardless of the color of their skin and texture of their hair and that is the Human Race. It does not matter what any man or woman looks like, due to the simple fact that he is a man and she is a woman, they possess the natural attributes of God, for Man was created in the image of God by The Creator Himself, which makes every human being part of the Human Race, period. Are there any hidden mysteries about the creation of man that I need to discover? Did God create three types of men, each individually given a different color of skin and put each them on separate parts of the world as a different race? I believe God did not create a white man and a black man or any other man so each could populate the earth categorically as three types of people. The biblical version states that God formed man out of dust. When God took a handful of dirt from the ground, it could have been any color depending on the soil of that region, and whatever the color was after God molded it with saliva, then that's the color of what was formed. Then Moses said God breathed into its nostrils the breath of life, and it, whatever was formed, became a living Being, which hence was named Adam, the Man. If so, then where did the human race distinction come from?

The evolution of skin types, skin colors, and hair textures must have started somewhere during the evolution of time, but the question is when, and how did it began, and what the original man looked like. When God created Adam, was he a white man or a black man or another color? Did the black evolve out of the white or was it the other way around? If there was any possibility of one color deriving from another, then

7

it would make more sense for me to believe that the white evolved out of the black. In other words, I'm saying that Adam the primary Man created, could have been a black man, and through him with Eve the world was populated.

In our modern world we witness how some of our black brothers and sisters have changed their color of skin to become white through surgical procedures, bleaching or skin discoloration. However I have never seen a white person become black neither surgically nor naturally. A white person can be tanned but eventually soon after, the natural skin color will reappear. A black carcass that has been hooked onto something under water for days could sometime be a puzzling task to discover its racial identity, because the water current washes the color off of it and it turns white or pale, which may also be caused by lack of blood circulation in the veins. In any case, none of that should matter to the point of propagandizing dogmas of superiority and inferiority among civilizations of our world, according to the color of skin of anyone or any group. All the confusions about race are man-theorized philosophies, terminologies invented to create differences of what someone should be perceived and identified as, which in turn makes it easier to impose inequality between men and women in a world made of all sorts of inestimable diversities.

I have also done some studies on how, when, and where the evolution of skin colors began, and as anyone would imagine, that was an idiotic thought to conceive, not to forget to mention a very difficult task to even think about trying to fulfill. There is no particular reason or time or place for such an occurrence other than when God created man in His own image, and because God is Spirit and thus has no physical appearance by which anyone could describe Him. God is an eternal spiritual Being with mighty powers, He could be anyone at any given time on any planet in the galaxy, including the planet Earth, and everywhere else all at the same time, for God is omnipresent.

Who can explain how there are so many different fish in the sea? They look different in sizes, in colors, and physical structures, the edible ones have different tastes, but all fish are originated out of one body, the Ocean. Who can explain the differences among the birds of the sky and of the fields? The parrots and the peacocks are admirable birds, but the crow is an eerie looking creature that depicts wickedness in the cinematographic industry, but they are all part of the same family, part of the bird race. How can someone perceive something one way and someone else sees that same thing in a contrary way? A woman may seem beautiful to one man and not so beautiful to another. Sometime it's all in the mind. Just like these questions, there are much more out there without definite answers. Professionals have been delegated by various government agencies of many powerful countries, to go above and beyond, searching for hypothetical facts in an effort to come up with answers to certain wonders. Some have gone and never made it back to earth, and those who are lucky to be alive or sane depending on their odyssey, they come back with artifacts and photographs, and propagandize their discoveries as genuine. But what may be believed to be genuine to them may not to be genuine to others, and I call them pseudo-propagandas about the origin of the human race and the planet Earth. All the proofs are right here on earth, but some of us never realize that. My perception is that a human being is a human being only to anyone who looks and feels and believes that he or she too is a human being. As we all or some of us may have heard that expression before, "it takes one to know one." An animal recognizes the characteristics of another of its kind, but humans created in the image of God with unlimited knowledge and comprehension of almost everything under the sky, still find it hard to accept and recognize that despite the color of our skin we are equivalent in human status.

The Beginning
and the fall of Mankind

The population of earth began by Adam and Eve, dwelling in the garden of Eden, from where they were cast out because of their disobedience. Their fall came about after Eve ate out of the fruit from a tree said to be located in the middle of the garden. That tree produces the fruit of knowledge, and they were forbidden to eat from it. Eve, who is thought to have been neurologically weaker as a woman, was the first to succumb into sinning. She was the first one to be tempted by the serpent in the garden. The serpent that has been primordially an angel, occupying the greatest position over all the angels in heaven, the one who covered the glory of God, the one angel named Lucifer who had zillion of angels under his command, became jealous of God and wanted to take God's deific position. Lucifer's beauty surpassed that of all angels in heaven, and he was the most powerful. Lucifer then convened with his angelic subjects and fanatics to battle with God for power, a battle he apparently lost, and they were precipitated out of heaven for eternity. Lucifer still beautiful in the face and irresistible by ways of expressing himself was full of charms and very cunning. He had appeared to Eve when she was alone and vulnerable in some part of the garden, indulging herself in God's glorious and lavish lifestyle that was created for them. Lucifer seduced

Eve, enticed her into doing exactly what God had forbade her and Adam to do, which was not to eat from the tree in the middle of the garden. She was deceived. The serpent gave her the fruit and seduced her into eating out of it. She then proceeded to bring the fruit to Adam who had eaten of it as well, even when he knew he wasn't supposed to, after God spoke to him personally about that particular tree, even before Eve was around. In all fairness to Eve, she wasn't personally told about the fruit, because she was not formed yet. It was up to Adam to tell her, but instead he decided to sin and spiritually die with her. This could actually be perceived as an act of unconditional love, where some people may feel that Adam loved Eve with such a passion that he was willing to go down that perilous path with her as one. But personally I feel that Adam is the one responsible for failure from the beginning of time, he had the truth, he knew what he was doing was mutiny against God, but he chose to do it anyway. I always wonder what if Adam had refrained from eating out of the fruit when Eve brought it to him, how would humanity be? Would every man still have that same cohesive and personal relationship that existed between God and Adam, and the women would not, because Eve sinned? Again this is another baffling question that should be reserved for a roundtable discussion. When they consumed the fruit of good and evil, not only they disobeyed God but they also acquired knowledge, the ability to differentiate right from wrong, and that's where the fall of man began. After God discovered what had happened, God pronounced sentences on the Man, Adam, saying with the sweats of his forehead and the work of his hands he shall eat and provide bread for his family. The Woman, Eve, shall induce great pain in laboring her baby.

Then upon Lucifer the serpent, God commanded from that day on that it crawls on its belly for the rest of its existence. Adam and Eve were forced out of the garden as they went into the wilderness where they were on their own for survival without the close relationship that formerly existed between them and God. They were alone, making all sorts of decisions, wrong and evil choices. They became immoral, arrogant, narcissistic, as evil took the greater portion of their heart. Cain, their first born murdered his brother Abel out of jealousy. That was the first murder, the first physical death on earth. Cain was also cursed by God and was completely isolated from the presence of God. Another question that I have been asking myself for years is that, two sons were born to Adam and Eve, and one of them died, therefore there were only three human beings left on earth who were Adam, Eve, and Cain. But the Bible says that Cain was driven away from God's presence and away from his parents, and resided in the land of Nod, east of the garden of Eden. Then the writer, Moses goes right on to say that Cain lay with his wife, his wife became pregnant and gave birth to a son they named Enoch. The question is, who was the forth person, the woman who became Cain's wife? Where did she come from? Then I came up with my own hypothesis that since Cain and his parents went asunder, over a period of time Adam and Eve must have had other children whom Cain was not around to know and live with, and therefore was not acquainted with. Thus I reached an understanding that it is very possible that Cain obviously got involved in a relationship with his parents' daughter and conceived children. They both did not know of the biological relationship between them, and therefore it was not considered immoral or sinful. That ancestral practice went on for centuries until the segregation of tribes came about, when relationship between two people was based on tribal and not on ancestral differences.

It appears that every research that has ever been conducted to locate the area where it's believed the Garden of Eden once situated leads to the east. In the book of Genesis, the first of five books written by Moses out of the sixty-six books of the Bible, he mentioned about four headwaters, the Pishon, the Gihon, the Tigris, and the Euphrates. Two of those rivers, the Pishon and the Gihon cannot be located, or they no longer exist due to erosions or other natural occurrences. However the Tigris and the Euphrates are currently on the map and they are identified by their ancient geographic names to this day. According to the location of those rivers' meeting point, the garden of Eden was in what is known today as the Southern Iraq. Extrapolating from the book of Genesis, the most reliable source on this matter to me, the east is the point from where the pervasion of man began.

The Regeneration
of the Human Race

Generations had past, they lived for hundreds of years, and then another man was born, and Noah was the name that was given to him. Noah himself had three sons, and their names were Shem, Ham, and Japheth. Men and women of that era continued on to live their sinful lifestyle, and so they were found to be perverted and corrupted in the eyes of the Creator. They were detested, and God saw that it was necessary to annihilate them. But Noah who was predestined for a very specific purpose, his life would be spared along with the rest of his family. God gave Noah strict instructions that he would build an ark, and how the ark was to be constructed. After that task was completed, days before the destruction, the ark was embarked with a pair of every creature, a male and a female, each after their own kind according to God's commands, with Noah and his wife, and their sons and their wives. Then came the deluge that wiped out the rest of humanity from earth. After the catastrophic inundation, only Noah and his family were protected and saved. Behold, a new pervasion of men began. The three sons of Noah, Shem, Ham and Japheth, by them in relations with their wives the earth was repopulated. That's why I believe we are all related, not by name or physical attributes alone but also by the origin of mankind. We are all of the source, we are all descendants of Adam and Eve and then of Noah. No man is naturally superior to another, superiority among humans can only be justified by knowledge, through which someone could be classified in a higher status in society, and by spirituality which directs the path of a man, causing him to live an ethical lifestyle which decides his destiny beyond the present life, and that's where the social level of one man may be superlative to that of another.

THE PERCEPTIONS OF SLAVERY

When the word slavery is spoken or heard, to some people it is a natural tendency to think that the context in which it is mentioned is about black people being manipulated and mistreated by white oppressors, especially someone who has been raised or being brought up in a black community, learning about black cultures and African histories. The reason for that is, as a child everything that was taught about black people and slavery in school or in a household, particularly in a country like Haiti which is mainly based on events involving a particular people who had fought their way out of servile bondage. Furthermore, Africa is known to be the place where the bulk of the slaves were taken and sold. For instance, in Haiti we are taught about our ancestors who were brought from Africa onto the land of Hispaniola were forced into slave labor. How they fought courageous battles against their white masters who oppressed them for years, battles that led them to be a victorious nation in 1804, and not just a nation but the First Black Republic in the world, and the first independent country in the Western hemisphere. We were brought up to believe that white men were our oppressors and adversaries. When we saw a white man on our street it was an unusual and appalling scene. If a black man was seen with a white man, although they may be friends who are just carrying a simple conversation while promenading the streets of Haiti, the natural instantaneous perception that takes no time to kick in is that the black man is a servant to the white man, or the white man is financially in a higher bracket compared to the black man, or the white man holds a higher position in the professional world juxtaposed to his friend with African background. That mentality would grow along with any child until a higher level of education is attained, from which that child may become more knowledgeable of certain events in history, and his mind may start to absorb fresh new and different ideas, which would lead to some truth and better understanding of some topics and events of the world. In due time that child who has grown in maturity, his mind becomes purged of all the negativities he's learned about what his ancestors have endured, which in consequence protect that person and others from the vindictiveness that once inflated his heart.

Indeed, slavery was not just a black or an African dilemma. From the end of the 16th century into the 17th century, slavery was not about race, gender, or culture, but it was about wealth and power, however religion did play a major part in it.

Many people who became slaves during that era were people who may have been captured as prisoners in battles between tribal rivalries, invasion of vulnerable villages, and at some point after a war between great empires. Some of them were not personally slaves, but they carried the servile status because their ancestors were captives of war. Sadly, historians reported that some were sold into slavery by their own parents in order to face extreme and deplorable conditions. A father would hand over one of his children for money or property, in order to take care of the others.

Another way a man may have become a slave was if he was convicted of a serious crime, he would be sold into slavery to compensate whoever was victimized by his criminal acts. Therefore anybody was prone to become a slave regardless of skin color or ethnic background.

Nobody was exempt from becoming a slave. It was about riches, power and honor, and so the strongest wins and takes all. At the end of a battle between two camps, the defeated side also loses their land and their freedom to their opponents who capture them, even if they simply became prizes of war. The prisoners would be dragged or sailed out of their territories and taken to estranged places, where the men would be exploited in doing heavy labors, as their women were found to be domesticated servants in wealthy households. The women were more lucrative in a way due to the fact that unlike the men they were utilized for purposes other than just house labor and cooking, etc. They were also exploited sexually or raped by their masters days in and days out. They would bear children who of course were not recognized to be the master's children; possibly in some cases they would abort the baby so they would not prolong the lineage of their misery by bringing children to their servile conditions. The African women were often transported to the neighboring countries like Syria and Arabia where they were sold to the Arabs, who then forced them into prostitution, which was also a very lucrative affair at that time and age. Even to this very day, despite the privileges that are available and offered to be moral professionals in most civilizations, there are people who still practice that same unethical lifestyle for survival, either on a personal level or under the control of a syndic for prostitution.

Although the job functions of these two characters may be parallel, there is a broad interval between a slave and a servant. With absolutely no perplexity, a slave is a person who is forced into a condition to perform unwilling and mostly undesirable tasks, someone who is treated like a property, someone who is deprived of liberty to operate as an individual with free will. In most cases a slave is treated in manners less than a domesticated animal which we refer to as pets now-a-days in households. Slaves are disrespected, whipped, with no exception of other types of ill treatments that they may endure at the hands of a master. On the other hand, someone could perform the same exact jobs of a slave and yet is not a slave but a servant. Being a servant is a condition that is usually chosen by will, and at any given time a servant may choose to suspend services and walk away and will not be detained or forced by anyone to stay. A servant is a person who has the liberty to go wherever, to do whatever, and be anything in society without being controlled or constrained by somebody else. A servant may also receive wages or some other type of compensation, whether it is accommodation, showing reciprocation for good deeds, or even monetary rewards according to what was discussed and concurred upon at the time of the initial agreement. A servant is not and cannot be considered a property of anyone, no price could be fixed upon a servant. A price can only be put on the services that a person provides.

Although slavery may be well alive de facto in some far away places, it has been abolished in the most part of the world. However it is ethically legal to employ a man or a woman as a servant, and they are found in wealthy households in America, in Europe, even in the Caribbean nations, they are simply referred to as maids or butlers, cooks, chefs, gardeners, nannies, or other titles they may be given according to what their job descriptions are. Servants do not suffer any hardship juxtaposed to what slaves underwent in previous ages, and that is a marvelous evolution since the servitude era back in the 16th and 17th centuries.

For forty years the Israelites were in bondage in Egypt. The Egyptians availed their strength and courage in the construction of great pyramids and breathtaking structures, some of which may still be standing steadfast to this day. Some people believe the pyramids were built through labors of free men, but if we sleep on it enough then we can arrive to other conclusions concerning that. The Hebrew went through the same mistreatments as well by the Egyptians. Their lamentations reached as far to the ears of God, and Moses was sent to deliver them out of bondage. But what many people may not know, is that the people of Israel were not captured, nor were they prisoners of war, but they gradually and voluntarily brought themselves into Egypt as servants to the Egyptians.

At first they were not considered slaves nor were they treated as such. It was a phase in their society when famine was ravaging their land, then Joseph the son of Jacob, who was sold into slavery by his brothers out of jealousy, found himself in the house of Potiphar, the captain of the guard under King Pharaoh. As believed, he was predestined to be the great man that he became during that epoch, and God utilized him for great revelations concerning the King and Egypt, and from that ability he obtained fame and power all over Egypt. By the second of the five years of famine in Israel, the Israelites started to succumb, and in exchange for food and lodgment, in diligence to secure their lives they ended up giving all of their possessions, their cattle, their land to Egypt, including themselves as servants and laborers in the care of the Egyptian monarchy. Life for them was in fact better. Joseph lived for a hundred and ten years and was buried in Egypt when he died.

The Bible does not specify neither genealogically nor by names how many and which kings reigned over Egypt, for they were all titled Pharaohs, and therefore we don't know which king was on power when Joseph died, but we can be sure that unlike his descendants he was well loved and was given an official and proper burial.

While the Israelites were in Egypt, they were multiplying in great quantities. The Egyptians felt threatened and intimidated in case of an uprising, thus the Israelites became detested by the Egyptians. They were soon spitefully forced into slavery, doing hard labor from dawn till dusk, living a brutal lifestyle for four seemingly infinite decades, until Moses led them out of Egypt.

So many families in the 1600s all the way through the 1800s found themselves in the same condition such as that of the Israelites, and they could have been anyone, of any ethnicity, whether they were Caucasian, Mongoloid, or Negroid.

Cohesive
Relationship of Mankind

Men were always intended to live in coherence with one another on one planet, speaking one language, and serving one God. It was not until the event of the Tower of Babel when God created confusion among the men, which caused them to disperse all over the earth.

The history behind the Tower of Babel explains how men conceived the idea of building a city, and in that city they would also build a tower that would be elevated to its pinnacle that the top of it would reach into heaven. The whole purpose behind that idea was mainly for men to create a name for themselves as the great architects, builders and inventors of time. The prophet said that the Lord came down among them and confounded their universal language, and they were no longer able to communicate with one another linguistically. It was a chaotic event. They were speaking in words which were not understood by one another, and therefore the construction of the Tower of Babel was ceased.

Men consequently went asunder, populating different regions with sons and daughters, speaking the languages that were bestowed upon them and their forefathers from that day. I believe that's where the variety of cultures came from, which eventually divided men into different groups and later became tribes, adopting different beliefs, creating a chain of religions which have great effect in societies even in nations around the world today.

It is not by chance that the people on earth have become the nations that they are. It is not by chance that we are the type of people that we are. The Creator was certain and positive of what He was doing in distributing what He has created to the heirs of His creation. It is not by chance that we speak different languages. We did not invent and develop these linguistic styles on our own, we simply learn from one another the languages that were bestowed upon us by God. We were and are still under the control of the supreme Being whose knowledge and power are superlative to ours. It is not by chance that Martin Luther King, Jr. became a vicarious figure to African descendants in America. It is not by chance that Barack Hussein Obama became the First African American President of the United States. Everything in life happens according to the supreme Being who is in absolute control of the world and the life of every man.

Although our physical eyes are not capable of seeing certain things and our human understanding is not capable of comprehending certain events and how they occur, there are many of us with the ability to discern occurrences and the chronological edict of events that are beyond our understanding.

You and I Belong Here

I adamantly believe that everyone is assigned to a land, a birthplace, and a people, even before naissance, and that no man is who he is at random or by chance. Behind each of us is an origin, a history that tells us about one another, and the various cultures that some of us may have adopted at a period of time in our life, for some particular reason or purpose. However nothing and I mean absolutely nothing can change anything about who we are naturally. Although the color of our skin may have different shades, the textures of our hairs and our physical appearances may differ, we are one Body, one People, and one human Race, originated from one Source. I believe it is about that time that we realize it and admit it, so we could move on with our lives toward a better direction for the sake of our future as a whole.

Today almost on every piece of land around the world is a particular people, and among that people can be found at least one man, a true patriot, who has become one with his land and his co-citizens, their cultures, their beliefs, and their lifestyles have become part of him. A country without at least one powerful man to love it, to care for it, to protect and defend it is a country in distress, with no hope, no future, but a path leading to the decimation of its own population. A country is a home to its nation, and without a country to call their own a nation is nomadic. A man who forgets or neglects his past, or one who is filled with shame about his origin is a homeless man with no historic values, who is always wandering and always being expedited from one place to another in dishonor and humiliation, to the point that even the values which he has previously acquired are reduced to nothing, and that man will eventually be degraded to the lowest point in social status. Just as our planet depends on all of us to be and remain a better living environment, a country as well depends on its people to manage it, to protect it from ruthless behaviors that would disable it from accomplishing one of its essential purposes, which is being a home, a safe abode for its inhabitants.

CHRISTOPHER COLUMBUS'
LIFE AND DISCOVERIES

On one of his voyages in search of a direct route from Europe to Asia, Christopher Columbus spotted the Americas, while sailing west across the Atlantic Ocean on October 12, 1492. No historian can give the exact place and date of birth of Christopher Columbus, however most scholars concluded that he was born on the port city of Genoa in Italy between August 25th and October 31st of 1451. He was the oldest of five children, with three brothers and one sister, Bartholomew, Giovanni Pellegrino, Giacomo, and Bianchinetta. In 1485, Christopher Columbus moved from Portugal to Spain. He could have had many children in various places since he has been aboard ships for numerous roles from the age of 14, and at 21 he became a privateer. However the two sons who were legitimately recognized to be his, since historians believe there could have been others, were Ferdinand Columbus, and Diego who was born to him by his wife Felipa Perestrello e Moniz.

Before his death in the city of Valladolid on May 20th1506, Christopher Columbus achieved four successful voyages to the Americas, mostly in the Caribbean, but the land of Hispaniola was definitely his favorite and that seems to have been his main base. He made frequent trips to Hispaniola. He would sail out for more discoveries elsewhere but then he would bounce right back to the island, to the point that on his fourth voyage King Ferdinand and Queen Isabella forbade him to go to Hispaniola, for things started to deteriorate due to poor leadership. The island of Hispaniola was the richest in the Caribbean, with an abundance of gold and natural minerals galore. Out of greed Christopher Columbus forced the inhabitants into servile labor in search of riches despite of his knowledge that Queen Isabella would disapprove of such act, and within a few days of excavation, about 22 lbs of precious minerals were collected. The people that were found on Hispaniola when Christopher Columbus disembarked there with his crew were the Tainos, and they called the Island Quisqueya, or Ayiti. Before Christopher Columbus left Quisqueya, he created a settlement made up of 39 of his crewmembers, and named it Navidad, which means Christmas or Noel. I'm thinking maybe the name derived from the time the settlement was created, which was possibly in the month of December, or it may have even been exactly on Christmas day.

From 1492 to the next 25 years, the island was under Spanish occupation, with a little over forty-five thousand Tainos who have endured and survived the treatments they were given by the Spaniards. Within many generations, the Taino survivors who either were victims of rape, or through concubinary relationships with the Spaniards and the African slaves who were brought onto the island, became biologically a multiethnic people.

By 1603, the French delegated colonists to occupy the north western part of Hispaniola. In 1697 the western third of Hispaniola which is now Haiti was in the possession of the French, the part of the island which they called Saint Domingue. Over the next century, that colony became one of the richest in the world and the richest in the Caribbean.

Slave Uprising

In 1791, during a revolution taking place in France, which was soon after entitled the French Revolution, disputes concurrently erupted among the whites and the mulattos in the French colony in Saint Domingue, which also led to a slave revolution. With Toussaint L'Ouverture, a former slave in his forties, who had joined the rebels as a medical officer, as head of the revolution, the spirits of the slaves fortified, united they fought a bloody battle against Napoleon and his troops, a battle which had vindicated their strength, the power of their intelligence, the resistance of their heart, and the determination for success in their relentless quest for freedom as black power and black roses. They found themselves in a constrained position that prevented them from exploiting their unique intrinsic values as valiant descendants of the great African nation, and most significantly as humans, as they were being exploited for their strong physical structure and energy to accelerate productions, and boost up the economy for then an unindustrialized world. It was about time they summoned the spirits they were introduced to by their forefathers to fight their oppression.

By the end of the 17th into the 18th century, Toussaint L'Ouverture and his followers claimed the whole island of

Hispaniola after Spain ceded the eastern portion of it, then the Spanish colony in Santo Domingo was also surrendered to the French in the Treaty of Basilea. In 1801, Napoleon Bonaparte sent his brother-in-law, General Charles Victor Emmanuel Leclerc, accompanied with about 20,000 troops to arrest Toussaint, reinstated slavery and reinforced French rule. Toussaint was deceived, captured on May 5, 1802, and was sent to France, where he perished in the frigid prison of Fort de Joux, in the Jura Mountains on April 7, 1803. However the fight continued with another valiant man, one of Toussaint's generals, a former slave himself, Jean-Jacques Dessalines. He ferociously led the final battle, defeated Napoleon forces who were said to die mostly of yellow fever, a disease from which General Leclerc himself also succumbed to and died in 1803. Leclerc's replacement General Donatien Rochambeau fought ridiculously to avert the fire that animated the slaves towards a definite victory, but again depleted with his troops and failed.

Even the very first president of the United States, George Washington, allocated almost half a million dollars in emergency assistance to the slave owners in Saint Domingue, as his right hand in Washington D.C, Thomas Jefferson, a slave owner himself dispensed thousands of dollars and hundreds of weapons to the French government, in diligence to keep the slaves in bondage. The slaves' independence disappointed the French, the Spaniards and the Americans; we must never believe for one second that those nations could ever truly be our friends or our allies. They do not indulge in our success of liberty, and if they had the chance we would be like Puerto Rico under their occupation once again like we were in 1915. Slavery was a very lucrative system that made their lazy lives easier, which put lots of money in their pockets, even when it was costing them thousands of lives of other human beings. I read an article that explained how three slaves were set aflame, one of them vociferated in agonizing pain as he burnt, another said to him with a fading voice, "Watch me now, I'm going to show you how to die." Then he just turned and embraced a nearby tree and burnt without a squeal, and one of the French men expounded, "This is the type of people we have to fight." In that same article I read as several children were on the verge of going through that same excruciating experience, as anyone would imagine they were petrified, and one of the mothers who were witnessing the inhumane ordeal murmured, "It is better to die as a slave then to live and see your children growing up in this condition."

The slaves though untrained and lightly armed unlike their adversaries, were not easy to beat, in their mind they visualized a better way of life, a greater and brighter future, they visualized a paradise island that the French and the Spaniards fought vehemently to maintain and control but defeated.

INDEPENDENCE DAY

On January 1,1804, the stupendous event that would shock the world finally took place, when General Dessalines declared the nation's independence, given the land its indigenous name Haiti, making it the First Black Republic in the world and the second independent nation in the western hemisphere.

Today on that island are two nations, on the western part are the bravest of all in the world, the Haitians, who have merited and earned the rights to live and function as an independent nation. On the eastern part of it are their co-habitants, the Dominicans who themselves from 1822-1844 were under the occupation of the Haitian government, until a heroic man by the name of Juan Pablo Duarte established the Republic of Saint Domingue an Independent State, which officially settled in 1865, now known as Dominican Republic. I have been thinking about it and I still can't comprehend how they managed to acquired a greater portion of the island, and I have a prescience that there may be a territorial war on the island between the two nations in the years to come. Over the years, Haitians who have been residing in Dominican Republic have not been treated fairly, and I believe it's a matter of time before the Haitians react, and no one knows what the outcome will be.

The Haitians are naturally a powerful people, with so much pride and histories which can neither be challenged nor taken away, nor could they ever be eradicated from their historic values. Those values were deemed by the lives of courageous men and women who gave themselves as sacrifices, who have sealed the proclamation of their independence with blood, shed blood of not regular men and women, but blood of valiant, determined patriots whose bodies and spirits led to an unforgettable victory, with historic prizes that will follow their sons and daughters throughout the world, in all civilizations, from generation to generations, even after the end of time itself. Therefore let it be known that we are a great nation. We have been raised in the eyes of all, and in the minds of the knowledgeable, in the face of those who are intelligent and wise enough to recognize greatness. Let it be known to the world what we are made of, what we are about and what we stand for, and that is Freedom. Regardless of the difficult periods we have endured, the circumstances we may be transcending, we must perceive them as different phases we need to experience so we could be mentally and physically stronger to encounter greater challenges, to fight for greater victories to come.

When I hear governments and citizens of other countries talking about their strong men and women, about people who are viewed as heroes in their country and communities, as I read and analyze the histories of my own people and their lives even to the present era, it is undoubtedly certain that the Haitians are indeed the strongest nation on earth. Their strength was not tested and displayed just for a particular period in history like the great civilizations and great powers of the past, but our centuries of endurance from then till now are evidence that we are still the strongest of them all.

While some are being succumbed to great powers, and others are selling their rights, their land and their freedom to foreign governments for citizenship, we the Haitians remain strong in our quest to sustain what are rightfully ours, which are our dignity and the land we call home, and most definitely to retain our liberty. In due time we will regain motivations and strength, to succeed in our wealth, in our economy, in building a bridge to a better life for our future generations, we did it once, and so we can and we will do it again and again, whenever it is necessary to be done, until we attain our essential goals, which is to pierce through the barriers of poverty, to regain true respect from the hypocritical nations around us.

First Black Nation in the World

To be the first is to be a leader, the one to get the first blow, the one who is likely the most intelligent, and the one who represents the rest, and in most cases the one whom others look up to and emulate. To be the first is to be an inspiration to those who feel uninspired, to convince a pessimist somewhere out there that anything is possible regardless of gender, physical aspect, or nationality.

The first of anything is always authentic and usually the best of its kind, the most significant, the most special, the most likely to be remembered, the one to go down in history for millenniums, to be left for future generations to study about. Who and how many people in America haven't heard of the Rev. Martin Luther King, Jr.? How many could say they haven't heard of Ghandy? Who haven't heard of Bob Marley, lord of reggae? Elvis Presley, lord of rock? Michael Jackson, lord of pop? Michael Jordan, lord on the basketball court? Pelle, Ronaldo, Maradona, lords on the soccer field, and Neil Armstrong, the first man to walk on the Moon in 1969. These personalities have penetrated the hearts and souls of men and women, young and old around the globe with words of their mouth, strokes of their pens, and what they can achieve with their God given gift of talents, that even after their time has expired, though they are no longer with us physically, they are still spoken of and heard about, adored, admired, even deified by some. But even to this day, some people have never heard of Haiti or its heroic histories, and the warriors who have made it a nation. Now-a-days the Haitians are known mostly for their economic struggle, their political weakness, their poverty, and their religious practices. When we browse for the meaning of voodoo on the internet, it is said to be originated from the island of Haiti. To many people the practice of voodoo may be perceived as a belief known to be inferior, or a religion on which the morale is based on hatred and immoral deeds. But to some it is a ritual practiced for healing, or a force that comes from the gods of the earth or the abyss, which is contrary and inferior to the divine power of God, which comes from above and goes beyond the metaphysics and comprehension of man. They are also recognized for their styles of music. However Haiti is inhabited by a diverse people, from complexions to social classes, knowledgeable personalities to baccalaureate scholars, to people who are blessed with all sorts of natural talents and skills, and syndicates who believe in various theories and practice many different faiths. That is my land, my place of birth, on which my umbilical cord was excised and buried, of which I am dearly proud, where my heart and my mind will always be, to which I will perpetually be loyal.

TRIAL ERA OF THE NATION

For over two decades the people of Haiti have been facing some very difficult times. Governments have come and gone with all the promises they made which they could not deliver, meanwhile the country remains in a ditch dug by previous regimes, and it has taken turn for the worse over the recent years. According to experiences, I have learned that people cannot depend and survive on promises alone. Promises are verbal or written statements made to support someone's hope for something to come, that may sometime be sealed by consequences if fail to meet. Promises are also spiritual or psychological hopes that someone possesses or gives to others as reassurances on a quest, a pursuit, a desire, or to proceed with life itself with the faith that things will eventually get better. But in today's most societies, we find many of our politicians making great promises through standing ovation worthy speeches, to catch the attention of the most vulnerable and naive groups, to get the votes of the population, but prove thereafter that all they actually had was simply an appearance and words of mouth, with big dreams and philosophies at least some of them, but indeed they are like monuments which have been sculpted into human forms, standing for something or even great deal of things, but indeed powerless, brainless, and thus futile to pursue and execute their promises. In the long run these politicians find themselves entangled in predicaments that only an impeachment or a Coup d'Etat could emancipate them from.

In Haiti too and mostly, we find those types of politicians, and it is more accessible for them in a country as such to penetrate the minds of the people and draw a multitude of followers, since the people of Haiti are in desperate needs, they long for a better way of life they hope someday to attain, which seems to be a very long way from where we are today. Sometime people need to put aside the books, the terminologies, forget about the speeches, and face the reality of actual events, and deal with them with natural responses and defenses. What the people of Haiti need in such difficult times is unity among themselves, and trust within one another. It's been said that the Haitians are not united, and that's one of their greatest downfalls, but I, as one of them resent this propaganda, for it has been vindicated that we do unify in due time, although sometimes our unification may be well to oust one of us who seems not to understand or care about the needy situations of the people, someone who is not mindful of the best interest of our country.

The problems the nation has been encountering are not political problems alone, their circumstances and conditions go far beyond what the constitutional laws might permit or forbid. In America for instance, the constitution allows a person to serve only two terms of four years as president. Whether that person may be the best thing that ever happens in the history of the American politics the constitution stands, and no one dares to contest it or try to override that part of it. The American people do have so many more candidates who indeed can do the job even better than others, and they too need to have their chances to execute their abilities and to share their ideas for the best of their country. However the Haitian people have never been ready for a democratic government, some people may be afraid to say it but let's face it, it's true.

Following all the years of trouble those people have subsisted, and they have longed for decades for a savior, if finally a true patriot comes along, someone who is pure at heart and sincere, a man with the flaming desire to lead the people of Haiti out of poverty to a better and secure life, I believe that eight years would not be sufficient for anybody to bring Haiti out of its deplorable conditions. I think it would be idiotic not to avail that opportunity and allow that person to follow through with his great plans for the country.

Therefore in cases like this, I believe the constitutional laws should be flexible, as long as it is for the best interest of not a particular group of people, but for a country and its citizens distinctively, respectively, and collectively.

A POLITICAL WORLD

I have heard a lot of negative statements about politics. Some citizens feel that politics is a filthy and unrighteous system, and they feel oblige to abstain themselves from it. Some have preached against it in religious congregations, constructing psychological barriers between politics and spirituality.

Politics is the science or art of government. To govern is to rule over a city, a country and its nation, to control public affairs, and to accommodate the essential needs of a nation.

Governmental policies and political differences have evolved into political instability. In a country like Haiti where there is a political struggle, there is always a national threat which has become a main concern to every citizen and foreign resident of the country. Some people feel that because they are not running for public affairs, or because they are not holding a position in the governmental pyramid, or because they don't belong to a particular political party, they are excluded from the political world. Their views of politics cannot be easily extracted from their mentality, however they need to be told they are politically incorrect, and that it is ignorant to have such a conception. In any civilization it is everybody's concern what goes on in the government. Politics is a system that is extremely fragile, and everything that's political is never minor. Any decision taken by those on power does have a tremendous effect on the people directly or indirectly, and sometime even the international population is affected. Politics is a system that concerns every citizen, every scholar, every child, every man and woman in any society regardless of ethnicity, religion, or how evasive someone may be about it. Anyone and everyone could easily be a success story or a tragic memory of politics one way or another.

Is it fair to stand by with arms crossed and watch loved ones or friends or your people being led deeper into misery and poverty, while some are being decimated, when there is a government elected and put in place to prevent exactly things of those sorts from happening? No, I just personally can't find myself doing that. I just can't be speechless and stagnant about such factors, for it is my business and my concerns like it's ought to be to everyone else. It is my propensity as a young patriot to challenge the web of situations in which my people have been caught. Anyone with the urge and the obligation to protect his family, to preserve his rights, to safeguard his reputation and his properties in a society is automatically involved in politics. I understand that political affairs may not be something some people want to be part of, then again who does have a choice to be or not to be part of it? That's where the standard of the human ways of life originated. It is the fundamental source of civilization, and therefore from the moment a child is born he or she enters a system of great inevitable challenges. Sooner or later that child as an adult, will be obliged to care for himself, to protect others, to love his family and his country, which leads to necessary actions to procure them, because it is the right thing to do, it is the probity of every man. Whether anyone believes it or not, it is a dimension the political evolution has taken, a political world which no citizen can escape.

VINDICATION

A great man who deserves gratitude for his surpassing role as the adamant leader in the American Civil Rights movement, the Reverend Martin Luther King Jr., has changed the American history about the way black people are perceived and treated in America, although there still is some resentment toward African children here in the United States, but at least it's not as vivid as it once was. The most astonishing march ever held in the country was on August 1963 in Washington D.C, where the Rev. gathered a stupendous multitude who had the chance to hear him deliver his most famous "I Have a Dream" speech. A dream in which he envisioned black boys and black girls holding hands harmoniously with white boys and white girls. His name and that speech resonated throughout the world. He knew deep down inside that his dream was going to take time with persistence and heavenly assistance to vivify, but he sought mightily to make that dream a reality by devoting his times and efforts, putting himself and his family in harms way, to the very moment when he inhaled his last breath in Tennessee on April 4,1968. That day, Martin Luther King Jr. was assassinated in the process of fulfilling that very vicarious dream. Though racism pervaded our planet in some form or another, the United States of America is the land on which the fire was first lit to abolish it.

Dr. Martin Luther King Jr. was not so fortunate to experience and enjoy the fruit of his own courageous deeds, but to us all he has left a priceless gift which had cost him everything, including his life. Thus, we all ought to be filled with gratitude as we avail every moment of this new era of our life. It's not ironic that the trace of racism can still be found among us, in someone's heart, deep within some misanthropes even here in America, and it would be naïve for anyone to think otherwise.

I have heard that if someone is called to be talesman and claims to be a racist, then that person would be exempt from serving jury duty. I thought someone would have to be overly audacious to openly claim to be a racist, but we do have people who have played that card and they have gotten out of jury duty with no action taken against them, like their admission of being racists is not a big deal at all. Now this is something to really worry about, a topic that needs to be addressed authoritatively.

I always wonder how different things would have been if Dr. Martin Luther King Jr. was still alive today? What would he say about the Sean Bell situation? How would he respond to the flood in Louisiana? Would he be nominated as a candidate to be the first African American president of the United States? Would he win? Would he be a deific role model in the African community? Then again I have realized no child is born without labor, no success is achieved without efforts. The greater value something has the greater is its cost. From the beginning of time no land has been conquered without bloodshed, no warrior is left unscarred, and the one who fights for a revolution is most of the times never survive to live and enjoy the fruit of his revolutionary success. That is a pattern that every great man who has been a stepping stone in society seems to have followed. No man has been able to break that pattern since Jesus Christ has done it over two thousand years ago, and that's only because He's God, and He could not live among us like He previously did, but had to ascend to His heavenly abode, the place which could be accommodated to His divine quality. Therefore, if Martin Luther King Jr. did not die in order to attain the necessary dimension that only death could accomplish, then his fights, his dreams, and his life struggles for what he believed in would probably not have been vindicated.

WE ARE HAITIANS, WE ARE GOLDEN

Even before the Civil Rights movement took place in America from 1861 through 1865, or in Spain from 1936 through 1939, the slaves on the island of Hispaniola, our forefathers, the warriors and the heroes of the Haitian nation had already paved the way to freedom, which would in one shape or form open doors for the emancipation of slaves all over. If there were a celebration through which the world would acknowledge heroes of the centuries and warriors of the ages, then we the Haitians would certainly be the leading nation parading the avenues with our bi-color flags floating in the air with the creed as is it inscribed: Liberty, Equality, and Fraternity, although some of us may not take those terminologies to heart. Then again such an event is far from reality, for people tend to be very selfish, and they do not appreciate the achievements of others. While each society is given praises to their heroes, talking about themselves in the universities, write about themselves in collegiate textbooks and in magazines etc., they never consider mentioning anything about our history and our values. Who we are and what we have procured mean absolutely nothing to them. In their didactic projects and movements, they promulgate our political downfalls, they depict all the negative aspects of Haiti and its people, and they excoriate our beliefs and our cultures, but they neglect the positive and the wonderful factors about us, and the great histories behind us. But I believe people may choose not to understand our struggle, or they may not want to acknowledge our strength and courage, but we, Haitians, should know who were are, what we are about. These acknowledgements should be wrapped around the shoulders of every Haitian woman as a shawl, on every Haitian man as a breastplate. It is our history, it was our victory, if we don't value it then certainly no one else will. If we can't understand the significance and the importance of what we have then no one else can. The history we have behind us is extremely valuable. We must treasure it in our heart wherever we are. We should always stand with our head erect, with pride, with respect and dignity, with reverence for one another, for we are one.

We are like leaves hanging from the branches of a tree, when the wind blows we all shiver. In the fall together we succumb and wither, but our source of life remains steadfast with our branches awaiting our fresh reappearance with a more vibrant beauty that will sparkle with the raindrops of spring. Together we are strong, together it's all possible just like it was against the French in 1803, against the Duvalier regimes in 1986, against the accusation of being the carrier of the AIDS virus in 1991, when the Brooklyn bridge shuddered under our feet.

We are Haitians, we can do anything, we can face anything, we can triumph and overcome anything, and we can achieve anything when we converge for a common purpose.

My Land

Since this is not an autobiography, I will try not to expose myself too much in this publication. However I feel it will be easier and more explicit for me to write about Haiti and my people from my own perspectives, extrapolating from my own knowledge and experiences.

One of my motives for being so determined to write this book, is to embolden my fellow Haitian patriots on their quest for a better Haiti and to become a peaceful nation, and most significantly for a brighter and secure future for every Haitian child, to be proud of their origin and culture, wherever they may be, on their homeland or abroad.

I was born in the country's capital Port-au-prince on August 17, 1976. Here I am 26 years later, writing a book about my beloved country and its struggling nation from which I have been away for over a decade now. Sometimes I feel that I am the most patriotic Haitian upon the surface of the earth. Over the past decades I have seen and heard many occurrences which have had great impact on my life. Those that made me content, those that brought me sorrow, those that persuaded me to understand certain factors, and those that have compelled me to have faith, to believe, and to pray with optimism. I've learned to be sincere and loving both to myself and others, to look at people and understand them beyond their physical aspect, their linguistic differences as well as their actions, knowing and remembering that there is more to a human being than what the eyes can see and what the mind can comprehend. I have discovered so much about myself along the way. But among all those things I have realized, there is one that marveled me the most and that's the incomparable affection I am filled with for Haiti. The love I find in my heart for that land is something I think no one would ever dream or imagine existed. On many nights and days I would find myself cogitating on the beautiful moments I've enjoyed there as a child, those memories are my strength and my hope, on which I find solace on a daily basis, to keep fighting and working and hoping for a politically sustained nation.

It hurts me profoundly that Haiti, the land on which I was given birth, and the people with whom I share my nationality and whose blood circulates through my veins, are experiencing difficulties as such as they have never experienced before.

MY STORY

Although I was too ignorant as a child to know or understand politics and many other life's factors, like most children, I too have collected and kept so much of my childhood memories. One of the pictures I have captured and have kept in my heart to this day is the fact that Haiti was once the most wonderful place I knew, a country that has captured many hearts by its beauty, to the point that even today in its most unpleasant condition, some people like myself have a great portion of our heart that is still loyal to it.

Reminiscing on one of our summer vacations, I was probably five years old, when my maternal grandfather and I were heading to Les Cayes, one of the exciting provincial regions to visit in Haiti. As we were en route, and looking out the windows of the bus, along one side of the road were trees which seemed to be moving toward the opposite direction as if I was watching a virtual reality production, as they rotate around each other as the bus rolled on. On the other side were sea boulders, and beyond them at a distance was the crystal blue water, with a couple of fishermen on their fishing boats and canoes, some with colorful and tropically painted shirt unbuttoned and waving in the wind, and some shirtless, with straw hat on protecting their eyes from the scorching sun. Those were amazing panoramic views that could broaden anyone's perceptions about life, the world and the Creator, how perfect God is in His creation of everything in existence, and I had so much fun just indulging myself in it.

My head was relentlessly turning from left to right, capturing the scenic activities as we listened to the best compositions of the greatest and prolific musicians and singers of the time. But soon after my eyes got weary as I succumbed to exhaustion and fell asleep.

Our Dishes

The buses would stop along the way at one of the most famous marketplaces familiar to all travelers heading west of the country from the capital, known as Kafou De Ruisso. In that marketplace, everyone can find something of interest to spend money on, but what the travelers enjoy the most are the appetizers. A variety of luscious dishes mostly fried foods, from fried fish to green plantain, fried pork, sausages, fried sweet potatoes, and what we call acra. Acra is simply fresh grated manioc, which is known in Hispanic term as cassava. They mix it with spices and hot pepper, cut into small pieces and placed in a pot of hot olive oil to be fried for about one minute. But a dish would be incomplete without the pikliz, which is a mixture of chopped vegetables like cabbage, carrots, and green or red hot peppers or both, saturated in vinegar over a period of time for better results in taste. Now that is a delectable dish.

Whatever you're craving for you will find it there. But for me a trip to and from the provinces would not be as pleasant if we didn't get some Dous Makros. It is some type of cake made with a special flour, it's made of several pieces of various colors aligned parallel as a whole. I think the colors alone make it very interesting and attractive to the eyes, especially to those of children. It tastes and melts deliciously on the tongue, and masticates with a delightful feeling between the teeth. Most Haitian travelers always bring a couple of pieces of that cake with them from a trip between the regions intersecting Kafou De Ruisso.

All along the way are natural and topographical structures that catch the eyes and the heart of sightseers in many different ways. Some of the mountains are elevated high and peak. The trees are fruitful, the birds have brilliant colorful plumage, and they are appealing to the imagination; the rivulets and the streams run in rhythmic current through rocky watercourses and canals. The plantations are green and fresh, the livestock are plentiful and healthy. The regional settlers come out and wave goodbye to travelers on autobuses as their dogs run out on the front lawn barking at unfamiliar faces.

I remember seeing a mother walking alongside a dirt road, her head wrapped in a colorful peasant bandana, clutching on to the bridle of a donkey. Sitting on the donkey was a beautiful girl between the ages of ten and twelve. Her eyes were as beautiful as the moon on an early summer night, her hair was softly blowing over her shoulders as the fresh early breeze flows around them. Wearing her primitively sewn navy blue robe with modesty, it brought to my attention that it's not the outfit which makes a person beautiful, but the beautiful person who wears it makes it look beautiful. A naturally beautiful woman could wrap herself in banana leaves and she would make it seem so a la mode that even Versace would feel incompetent in his designs. The appearance of her innocent countenance as she's sitting on the surcingle and being ridden on a donkey was beyond captivating. Then I realize how a beauty as such would motivate someone to work adamantly hard to create a better environment, to contrive a better living condition with love and care for our young boys and girls, for them to have a chance to exploit and expose their talents, their beauty and their intrinsic values as human beings impeccably made in the image of God, as progenies of Haitian warriors and their queens.

Contemplating on the fun I was anticipating on having as I remembered of my previous trip to the provinces, I was already living it. Gorging on some griot and acra with a bottle of cola in one hand, listening to some compas music that made even my toes dance, as fresh air blowing in through the windows of the autobus and around my ears. That was just the beginning of the fun I was about to experience.

The people in the countryside are distinctively kind and courteous unlike most of those in the cities. They are full of great characters that give outsiders a taste of what savoir vivre really means. I was overwhelmed with envy to stay among them by their wonderful ways of embracing life.

LIFE IN THE PROVINCES

My great grandfather's bungalow was surrounded by different fruit-bearing trees like cocoa, coffee, papaya and different types of mangoes as the list goes on. Many of those countrymen are mostly specialized in tobacco growth. For that purpose, a barn is built next to almost every house. They would hang the fresh tobacco in the barn for a period of time until it is completely dried, in which state it turns brown and ready to be utilized. Then it would either be shipped to cigar manufactures in the neighboring regions, or to be sold in retail amounts to merchants in the area. For some perplex reasons the barn is always constructed to exceed the size of the residential structure next to which it is built by both height and width.

About fifty feet from my great grandparent's house is a stream of fresh water running from a cascade one house up that belongs to my great uncle, who was a law enforcement officer in the area. Across the stream is a non-asphalted road. Looking beyond the stream and the rough road is a mountain gradually elevated from the left side to the other, and as it prolongs to about a quarter of a mile to the other side, it reaches approximately one hundred feet in altitude. The air in the countryside as most people would imagine is definitely fresher and cleaner compared to that in the city. Standing on a mountaintop and looking down from miles away over the vast green land pervaded with livestock, and birds flying between the clouds under the blue background, are views that are remarkably indulging, panoramas that famous artists would love to depict in their paintings for lucrative marketing.

It was around six in the evening when we arrived at the provincial city of Les Cayes. The roosters were getting ready to fly up the tree branches for the night. The bulls and all the livestock and domesticated animals were secured in their pastures and stables. The farmers were beginning to retire from a hard day of labor. When we stepped out of the car, a group of family members accompanied by some curious neighbors and others who claimed to be distant relatives of ours ran forward to meet us joyfully as they embraced us like lost sons of a king. A couple of dogs waggling their tails awaiting impatiently on the opposite side of the stream, with their ears erect waiting to sniff on us. We crossed over, some of them carrying our baggage, those with sympathetic expressions on their face for my grandfather who had lost his youngest daughter, my mother, whom my presence reminded them of.

My great grandmother was still alive at the time, but in her old days and bed ridden for she was blind. We strolled down by her bedside to greet her. She reciprocated with a great smile as she hugged and kissed and touched my grandpa's hairy cheeks and chin. Attentive to my voice, she slowly turned to the left reaching out trying to touch my little smooth baby face saying, "Where's my baby." I stood up on a stool trying to reach the height of the bed so she didn't have to strain out her arm; my grandfather helped me up the bed to her reach. She started feeling on my little hands and arms and finally touched my face; her hand felt so tender. She was lying there so beautifully on her antique oversized bed with a giant headboard. Her gray hair covering her ears, with her arm around my tiny waist. Her face was full of reverence, angelic and pure. It was a moment of loving expressions that would bring smiles on the face of any child, and contentment in the heart of any grandchild.

They began to get into some deep conversation, you know how those ancient ones always have some old time stories to tell when they live through so many decades, and only senile dementia would protect someone from having to hear all the experiences of their lifetime. Thus, my great grandfather came to emancipate us from the tight grip of his wife, telling her that we just got there and we're hungry, to let us go and eat.

As he led us to the dining table, a lady approached with a vessel of water and a towel proportionally hung from her left shoulder. My grandpa washed his hands and then mines, and wiped them off with the towel. As we sat on the table, the delicate scent coming into my nostrils was so appetizing I started to salivate. My grandpa set me a plate; I ate like a little gourmand as usual. I was a greedy kid, I was always chubby, until I was about twelve or thirteen years old when I started to be conscious of my body. The chicken bone was so scrumptious that I chewed on the soft part until I drained the sauce out of it. That was a real treat.

A couple of hours later I was all excited to go on a promenade in the neighborhood with a group of older relatives. They introduced me to some other relatives who were glad to know and meet me for the first time. Those who presented me with chicken eggs and others with whatever they had lying around, it's always been said that it's the thought that counts. But let me just say that it's awkward what they would give somebody as a present. It would not be unusual for them to tie a string around a chicken's foot and hand it to you as a present, or a rope around a piglet's neck and say, I have nothing to give you my son but here, take this piglet, in a couple of years it will be ready for a feast.

On our way back home, I grabbed some guava fresh off the trees and ate along the way. When we got back to the house, I handed what I have received over to my grandpa. Then we went for a swim under the waterfall despite that the clouds were condensing and merging for an outpour. The sound of the cascading water was like music to my ears, it was very amusing, although the water was precipitating hard and tingly on my young and fragile body. It started to rain, but we lingered in the water for a little while. Soon after we ran back to the barn where my great grandfather and grandpa were sitting and chatting. Around them were baskets of delicious looking mangoes of all kinds. I went and sat adjacently to them. I dug in the baskets like I have never seen mangoes in my life before. Curious to find out what they distinctively tasted like, before I could finish one I tossed it aside and started on an other. I peeled and ate so many of them until I couldn't eat anymore. My grandfathers didn't complain one bit, mangoes were not scarce at all in those days, they were found all over the place rotten and stepped on, that's how it's always been in the provinces, at least that how I remembered it to be then. Mangoes are the most prolific fruits in Haiti. Even here in the United States, mangoes from Haiti are known to be the sweetest and the most succulent of them all. When my grandfather finally realized my greediness over the mangoes it was too late. My stomach was already feeling squeamish and upsetting. He saw the grimace on my face and told me to slow down but I was feeling drowsy and was ready to turn in. The rain subsided and I walked to the stream and washed my lips and hands. I then strolled to a room and struggled up to another oversized bed from where I could only manage to watch the other kids play, but too bloated and uncomfortable to join them. About five minutes after, my grandfathers rushed into the house through the rain which had restarted to precipitate harder than before, trying to elude giant blood-thirsty mosquitoes.

The raindrops hitting the corrugated iron used as roofing on the house, for those who haven't had that experience, I must tell you it's a great feeling, a moment that could be unforgettably romantic for two people who are passionately in love. If attentively listening to the echoes of the raindrops on the rooftop, you could actually hear it like a melody being played by nature. Depending on the quantity and the velocity of the raindrops concomitant with the wind, and the voices of people trying to communicate through the echo, it is an experience like no other. On a rainy day as such is when I have my best sleep.

The next morning I was awaken to the crow of the roosters, signifying the rising of the sun above the horizon which is around six o'clock in the morning. By then the elders were up and active, preparing breakfast before everyone else awakes. By the time I was up everything was ready, the wonderful smell of coffee and fried eggs just pervaded the house. As I stood on the porch inhaling the fresh morning breeze, I saw the merchants passing by on their way to the marketplace, carrying baskets on their heads or shoulders. Those who carried fruits in varieties like bananas, apricots, oranges, lychees, pineapples, and papayas just to name a few. Those with fresh vegetables and others with hot freshly baked bread. A man would come by every morning at dawn, delivering fresh milk on subscription to neighborhood consumers. Everything is all fresh, and that definitely makes a real difference on the taste and certainly on the nutritive values compared to frozen foods or those with preservatives found in the metropolis.

The provincial lifestyle may have its disadvantages as opposed to that of the city when it comes to educational and social aspects, however once it becomes part of you and you begin to adapt to it, it's a lifestyle that could be hard to trade. Although I was starting to develop some love for it I could never get too attached, because I always had to go back to Port-au-prince for school, which was another adventure for me. That is just to share a succinct part of my voluminous memoirs of how Haiti was at some point, and meant to so many of us. These are unforgettable events and experiences we can take with us, in our heart and in our memories, anywhere we go, beyond the ocean, onto foreign lands and other civilizations, to bring us back home whenever we want in our own psychological world.

My Grandfather's Operation

Just when I was getting acquainted with new people and more of my family members, I was looking forward to enjoy my summer vacation in the province in its fullness, but my life was about to take a cataclysmic turn that would change everything. My grandfather was suffering from a sickness that was oblivious to me, for I was just a little boy, I never saw or heard him talking about it nor did I ever see him suffering from it. While we were on vacation in the countryside, he decided to go for an operation, possibly due to the fact that his sickness was taking course for the worse, or the operation was long overdue. Young and ignorant I was on certain aspects of life, not knowing the severity of his illness, everything seemed normal and usual to me like every other day. But on a bright sunny and breezy afternoon, everything seemed calm, the air was dry, there were no birds in the sky. My world seemed gloomy, nothing and no one was able to bring a smile on my face, I was missing him dearly for the whole duration he was in the hospital, and I couldn't wait any longer for him to come back. That was actually the very first time I was without him for such a long period of time, the first time I remembered ever felt so lonely, and I sensed that my life once again was about to take a blow which would change my perceptions forever. Later on that day everybody sat around waiting impatiently, we saw the car that my grandfather's brother owned approaching, the one who is also a law enforcer in the region. When we saw the car coming, our heart unclenched and we started to rejoice, but our songs of joy abruptly turned into excruciating sorrow when we looked in the car and saw the expressions on the countenances of those who had gone to see my grandfather in the hospital. So one of the elders inquired about his recovery status, no one responded for a while, and then someone burst out in tears as another mumbled the operation was not successful. My grandfather was gone. People went in disarray. Someone grabbed me, lifted me up to his chest and clung onto me as he squealed out his name, asking why? Still I didn't really grasp the full impact of the announcement, but overwhelmed by emotions with all those people around me screaming my grandfather's name with gushing tears, and I started to cry as well. Unlike the death of my mother which had no mental and emotional effects on me because I was a baby when she left me, my grandfather's passing was different. I was old enough to know something extremely wrong had happened, and it was heart wrenching. Ironically it was the last time we would ever be together, just the two of us, but the memories are inescapable. Those who knew him, and who have heard him speaking of me, they knew that my life and my future were going to be precarious without him. He would have done everything in his power for me to become the man I'm supposed to be. He created a beautiful life for me in his mind, and made it vivid through his words and expressions. The love he had for me was easy to see, and the values he'd shown toward me were instilled in me.

My grandfather was laid to rest in a tomb painted in sky blue on top of a mountain nearby a major roadway. Every time

I go there to see my family, which is rare, all I have to do is look up toward that mountaintop and there is the blue tomb reminding me of great times which always quickly turn into sadness and nostalgia.

My Introduction to a New Life

After the passing of my grandfather, I became nomadic for the next several years. I must have been about seven years old going on eight when my grandfather died. Since our distant relatives in the countryside were not really familiar with the city life, and they had no kind of contact with the rest of the family in the capital, I ended up getting stranded in the province with family members I barely knew. I was taken in by my grandfather's older brother who had a family of his own, his wife and their seven children. They were one of the very wealthy families in the region where they lived. He was known as a successful agriculturist. I stayed with them for about two years, living a life I was in fact unfamiliar with, and it was really difficult for me to comprehend and accept the sudden change, and I had no choice but to adapt to it. Dwelling under the same roof with nine people who were virtually strangers to me, each with a different personality and attitude, indeed was a drastic transition in my life, when it was I and my grandfather who lived in a one bedroom apartment in the capital, and my caretaker who sporadically slept over when my grandfather would go out of town. The two youngest of his children, a girl and a boy who were in my age group, were my closest acquaintances who didn't make me feel entirely left out, but even them too seemed estrange to me. Up to that point it never occurred to me that there were such connections as maternal and paternal relationships, for the only person I ever knew and was attached to was my grandfather. Therefore I never bothered to inquire about my mother or my father, whether they were dead or alive. But subconsciously I felt there were things I wanted to know about, living with such a large family somehow caught my attention, but I didn't really contemplate on it like it was of any importance to me. I was just going through life one day at a time, waiting for something to happen, longing for a change. Although I didn't know exactly what I wanted to happen, I simply kept hoping for something, because I believed nothing could have been worse than what I was already enduring.

The two youngest children and I were often accompanied to the provincial city either on vacation, or when the father went on business trips. Like all kids, we enjoyed the traveling experience.

Meeting My Maternal Aunt

During our sojourn there, we would dwell in a house located by the main bus station, from which people could find buses departing to various parts of the country, and so we were seeing innumerable faces on a daily basis. There, were some paternal relatives who lived nearby, but they weren't known to be related to me and I didn't know them neither. They were following my whereabouts subtly and reported to my father whom I had yet to know or meet.

One early morning just after breakfast, there was a knock on the front door. Since I was the closest to it, I proceeded with hesitation for I was a timid child, from the dining room which is located in the back of the house; I strolled through the living room and opened it. Standing there was a lady whom I could not have described with precision instantaneously, I never seen here before, but somehow her presence had an effect on me which had caused me to feel a bit mentally disoriented. Her facial expressions were disturbing, I guess it's because she knew who I was as soon as she saw me and that wasn't the case on my part. She had a smile on her face that got me wondering in perplexity. She said, "Good morning Kenzie". Kenzy was just a nickname by which my grandfather called me. When she said my name suddenly I was anesthetized, I stood there stagnant wondering how she knew me. Before I could even respond to her greeting my great uncle came to find out who was at the door I was talking to. She introduced herself to him claiming that she's Adeline's older sister. The name Adeline sounded familiar to me, Adeline was my mother. After hearing that, my great uncle invited her in to converse in elaboration. She started by saying how she's heard of me but had never met me before, and then after she had learned of my mother's passing it became a burden to her that she looks for me.

As everyone knew, my grandfather was overly protective of me, no one and not even my aunts and uncles, his own children were allowed to come near me. One of them who usually came by to see me sometimes would always come in the absence of my grandfather, her father, and she would plead to the neighbors and my caretaker not to tell my grandfather that she'd come by, because he would get very upset about it, and he would go to the extreme to make sure that he gets his way, that's how strict my grandfather was, and he got their respect. Sitting in the living room with my grandfather's bother, the lady went on to explain how she was waiting for that day to come, for she's barren and she wanted to adopt me as her own son. When she said that, there was this aura in the room, everyone was astonished. I was sitting in a chair with my head bowed, I felt tormented, it was like I was being held under water by a sack of pebbles with a rope tied around my ankles, and I was suffocating. I didn't know how to react to everything that was going on in that room, but I wished it wasn't happening and I wanted it to cease. All I wanted to do was run out of the house and find a secluded place to be all by myself. The tension started to mount between her and my great uncle in an aggressive manner.

As a woman that lady was determined and defensive, her aggressiveness brought a new perception to the household, because none of us had ever witnessed anyone talking in that tone to him before, although she was on their turf, all by herself against them all she was still fearless and outspoken. Like my grandfather, that man was stern and intimidating even to his own kids. His wife was a Christian lady who lived by the Holy Scriptures, and the commands of her husband. None of his children dared to step up to him, he had them living in complete fear under strict discipline. He and the lady exchanged vicious words as his wife and kids got involved, verbally ganging up on the lady. They were about to force her out of the house when she decided to leave voluntarily, but she warned them that she would be back soon, and the next time she would not be alone. All was occurring so fast right before my eyes. I was transfixed by the commotion, and it was all about me, I felt humiliated. It was one of the most confusing moments I ever had to cope with in that period of my life.

A couple of days later, I was politely dressed up, looking well cared for and protected. The next thing I knew I was sitting in a court room, being interrogated by a judge on whom I wanted to live with. I sat there in disadvantage to both parties, knowing absolutely nothing about this lady who's ready to just take me away with her, to wherever; then again living with my great uncle and his family was not a condition I was pleased with. I shared a bed with their youngest son who drenched it with urine every night, and every morning I was the one to be inculpated for it. No one stood up to admit that it was their son or brother who was doing it, that was exasperating to me. As I sat there in the courtroom, I felt weary, weary about the decision I was about to make, not knowing about what would be best for me. For I already knew what living with my great uncle and his family was like, I was already adapted to a lifestyle I knew of, although it wasn't the best, but I didn't know anything about my aunt, and I certainly didn't know how my life was going to be living with her. It would probably be better, or it would probably be worse. Finally, the verdict was pronounced. It was taken into consideration that my aunt was barren, and my great uncle and his wife were settled with a family of seven children of their own, and therefore my aunt was given custody over me. The outcome was devastating to both me and the family I was on the verge of leaving behind, as I witnessed the two youngest kids weeping. Although I was discontent living with them, it was still hard to go on without them. I was still skeptical to face the transition I was about to make. I left the courthouse hand in hand with a complete stranger, having no idea where life was about to take me, and what was waiting for me ahead.

LIVING WITH MY AUNT

It was an exhausting day for both of us but also a victorious one for my aunt after a hard fought battle, and therefore we didn't really get to develop a real conversation, besides, I had no idea who she was and thus had nothing to talk to her about, I assume she felt the same way. We arrived at her house about half an hour away from where I previously resided by the bus station, where she came to meet me. As we entered her residence, her neighbors on both sides stood by looking on and greeting me as she introduced me as her son. She sat me down in the center of a twin size bed placed adjacently to the front door and a side door which was also ajar to allow fresh air to penetrate the living room. She took off my shoes, placed them beneath the bed as accustomed. She strolled to the back of the house which I had yet to tour. Then she came back with a tin plate, she got my legs astride and placed the plate between them. The food I was served was not extraordinary as you may be waiting to read about, and I can't manage to keep a serious face writing about it. After all she went through just to have me in her life, the emotional moments we shared, the tears she shed, and the loyalty she showed toward me, I really was expecting a feast, but a feast was far from what I got. When I looked in the plate I saw boiled green bananas smeared with hot olive oil, with a little bit of salt and chopped scallions. No meat at all, not even chicken feet. However I was surprised by the taste of it. Do not judge the food by its description or appearance, it was ironically tasty beyond expectation. Then she brought a glass of home made lemonade, and she sat across from me with a smile on her face, as I fell deeper into discomfort at each glance I take in her direction. I was surrounded by all types of strange faces; they were being too nice to me that I started to get annoyed and worried about my safety. There were women in their thirties referring to me as, "My boyfriend" or "My future husband." Some kept saying tautologically that I was cute and other things that I was flattered to hear but I was still reluctant to crack a smile. Then I thought to myself, that wasn't so bad after all. I struggled through the day, and when the sun finally went down I thanked God that it was about to be over, hoping that once I laid my head to sleep I would wake up the next day ready to face my new environment.

My first night in that house was awkward; I was trying hard to keep my eyes open, trying to stay vigilant for as long as I could. I was thinking that her story could have been fabricated, she could have possibly been an impersonator taking advantage of a poor vulnerable orphan for whatever her exploitation may have been, in fact things like that are possible. But as vigilant as I wanted to be, as soon as I finally laid my head to a pillow, I was out like a light. The next day I was awaken to a sunshine bright morning, in a new home, a new environment, looking forward to new challenges in my life.

My aunt is indeed a woman of great character. She is a woman who is full of strength, a woman I classify as one of the true Haitian women. She possesses a love for me that is juxtaposed to that of my own mother. She too, like my grandfather, believes in me wholeheartedly with everything she's got.

My aunt and I experienced a great journey together, which had brought us closer to each other over the years I lived with her. With her I visited some parts of Haiti that are so secluded and consequently neglected, places that ninety percent of my peers have never been to or even heard of. There's a region named Les Anglais, which simply means The English. It is one town away from the borderland of Haiti and the Caribbean Sea on the south western part of the country. It's like a society in a whole world by itself, where the people have their sub-governmental system, and their own lifestyle and culture, like they have never been to, or even heard of any other places out there. That region is a very spooky place as well. It is so isolated that it has become an abode to those who practice witchcraft and voodoo abroad daylight.

There I have seen on many occasions, men and woman who have been turned into zombies, which is a state when someone's spirit has been summoned out of his body, and he becomes just an animated being with no ability to reason, with no control over his body, and oblivious to his surrounding. He wouldn't even know who he is, or where he comes from, or who his family is, he wouldn't even know his name. The spirit which has been extracted from one body could be summoned into someone else's body, or it could just be out there wandering until it finds a window to penetrate another body that had been left unoccupied, again by some satanic process.

On another occasion when I was there, I remember there was a school girl who was afraid to walk down the path that leads to her house, because of a neighborhood dog that was nearby. Being a nice boy trying to show my gallantry although I was afraid of dogs myself, and since I knew the dog which I have been around numerous times before, I figure the dog and I were on the same page. So I took her by the hand and walked her past the female dog which was lying on the floor nursing her young. She said thank you and she kept going on her way. As soon as I turned around to walk back home, the dog struck me once on my left leg, and then retreated on her own. That was one of the amazing things I have never witnessed before, and I kept asking myself what had happened, and I realized she was trying to protect he offspring. From that day on, I stayed away from that particular dog and every other dog, no matter how cute they are, or how innocent and docile their owners portrait them to be. Everything about the people of Les Anglais and their neighboring places is different from the rest of the population. Their life is so limited, deprived of what we may call essentials, and that causes me to wonder how they manage to subsist in such deplorable conditions all these years, but yet beautiful, interesting and historical. But those are some of the attributes that make Haiti and its people so promiscuous in social classes, in styles, in beliefs, in skills and talents, which make them very difficult to estimate. They are surviving and still subsisting through some distressful situations, that Americans and great nations of other industrialized and technologically advanced countries would not be able to withstand, to the point of asking themselves like I too ask myself many times, how do they do it?

Another occurrence that has remained mysterious to me even now is how my aunt had believed and testified to others, that my presence in her house had chased away the spirit of sterility. For many years she was in a concubinary relationship with a man who had been separated from his legitimate wife, after she had gone abroad. My aunt adamantly tried everything in her power, medically or culturally, to conceive a child, but she always ended up having a miscarriage. Ironically, while I was living with her she gave birth to a son, and since then she's been having fun, and had given birth to about six more children, with the oldest being in his early twenties now, and she feels that my presence in her home really had something to do with it.

My Belief Conquers My Fear

Strange things had happened, especially in those early years in my life. When I moved from my great uncle's house, I was hoping that things would be better than they had been previously. I was optimistic that if there was indeed a god or some type of supernatural force out there that my life would be taking in consideration, and whoever that god is or that force may be, it would show compassion toward me and bring me solace when I felt I needed it the most. I felt weary and perplexed and disoriented, but what scared me the most was the feeling of another major event I intuitively knew was about to occur, and I was afraid of facing it, since there seemed to have been a pattern of unsettlement and bad aura in my life. I must say in all seriousness that I was always a strong believer in someone or something stronger than us out there, something that is above all, or someone whose power and righteousness surpass ours, something by what a human being could be justified, someone by whom every man could be judged, and most importantly to whom or what we could go in our times of distress and know for certain that we will not be rebuked, but we will be embraced with open arms and love and compassion.

I always felt there was something in the air, something out there that is greater than life itself, that was watching over my every step in life. That force or whatever it may have been, that spiritual being, whoever he or it was, walked alongside me so patiently, to the point where I was able to trust it, and that's when I began to feel a little hopeful and courageous. It was like a burden was taking off my shoulders by simply making that force responsible for whatever would happen to me. In other words, I trust it to the point of putting it in charge of my destiny, because I believed in its prescient power to know and procure and accomplish what were beyond my abilities.

Thus, I began to feel the optimism, and I was looking forward steadfast to face whatever challenges I was about to encounter.

Later in those years I realized not what but who that person is, and by which name He should be referred to, and He is God, my God, whom some call Jehovah. The name Jehovah may be followed by other meaningful Hebraic terms to specify a plea depending on particular circumstances of a believer.

Here are some instances of the many names God is referred by to different people according to their cultures and their need of someone greater from which they seek refuge. Jehovah Nissi- Lord my banner; Jehovah Jireh- Lord will provide; Jehovah Tsidkenu- Lord our righteousness; Jehovah Rapha- Lord who heals; Jehovah Raah- Lord our shepherd; Jehovah Shalom- Lord our peace; and Jehovah Shammah- the Lord is present.

Recapitulating on those days in my life, if I was to personally adopt any of those terms, they would have been Jehovah Raah and Jehovah Shammah. Despite my ignorance, not knowing exactly who He was at that time, whether He was a physical being or a supernatural force, I always believed in His existence. Although I felt I was alone and lost in this world and in despair, I was never afraid of anything; I always felt strong and relentless, empowered and embolden in the midst of my circumstances.

Special Encounter

As years went by, history repeated itself in like manner in which I met my aunt. But this time it was someone else, a personality who is important and imperative in the life and future of every child, someone who has become one of the dearest individuals in my life. Although he was not there for me during the first eleven years of my life, and that unlike his other two children with his wife, I was expatriated after only four years of knowing him. Despite it all, the psychological pain he's caused me over the years which I'm still trying to cope with, he has remained an important personality to me, a part of me I can't neglect or escape even if I would want to.

My aunt and I arrived from one of our trips to Les Anglais one day, one of our neighbors who live right next door came over and told my aunt that three men had come by, and they went around asking questions concerning our whereabouts, and they wanted to know an approximate time when we were expected to come back. The men were told that we were out of town, and our return was precarious. They left after saying that they would be coming back sometime later on that month, and that my aunt should wait for them. A visit from some strangers leaving a message like that was nerve-racking to my aunt of course. However it was something we had to face eventually, in order to know who they were and what they were there for.

Approximately two weeks later, my aunt had sent me out on some errands, when I got back, there was a pickup truck parked on the street in front of the house, which was unusual, because my aunt didn't have friends with cars that came by sporadically without me knowing about it. As I approached the front porch entering the house, there were three men sitting in the living room. My aunt was sitting across from them, and her first biological son who was about three years old stood at the doorway looking on ambiguously. I walked in the room, I remarked the expression on her face, and I had a sense that something peculiar was in progress. One of the men was apparently older than the others; he was of the same complexion as one of the other two. I found out later that the two guys of the same complexion were father and son, uncle and cousin to the third man who had a darker complexion. All three of them had a delightful smile on the countenances, but the dark skinned one seemed to have more of an interest in me. Then I realized that the presence of those men meant something great, or maybe not so great, but definitely something out of the ordinary. They looked different, they spoke differently, and everything about them was dissimilar to us in that region in a more advanced way.

My aunt went right ahead and introduced me to them. But even before I could extend my hand, the older gentleman said, "There goes your boy," and I saw a radiant look in the face of the man with the most interest in me. He smiled at me as he responded "Yes indeed, this is my boy." He pulled me up closer to him, rubbed my head once, and sat me lightly on his lap facing the other men on his right. I looked at my aunt in astonishment, like, who the hell are these guys? I assumed she interpreted the perplexed expression on my face and my gesticulation, and then she bluntly said the man who was holding me was actually my father.

Suddenly I was feeling more uncomfortable. I squirted myself from under his arm. He turned his head and looked at me with flattery; he brushed his hand off my head again. It did not take long for my aunt, his uncle, and cousin to conclude that there was indeed a resemblance between us as father and son, though our complexions differ.

My aunt fell in despair, thinking she was about to lose me, but he reassured her that he's not there to alienate me from her, but simply to introduce me to a better lifestyle contrary to that of the province, and expose me to a better environment and a more suitable educational system. After a detailed and lengthy discussion about what the future may hold for me that my father had resurfaced into my life after eleven years, suddenly I began to transition from my previous attitude and mental state. I knew then I have a father whom I just reconciled with at last. No one would imagine the transformation that I felt innately, which radiated all around me. And from that day on I was a different person. I became mentally strong, I began to feel positive about myself. I started to walk with my head up, feeling my days of mourning caused by not knowing my biological parents were over. Still I didn't have any idea about my deceased mother, and so it didn't really bother me, therefore the presence of my father was sufficed to take the next step in my life.

After some intense negotiation, my father was given the green light to take me with him to the capital. However I had to remain in the province with my aunt a little longer, before the initiative could be finalized. Assumingly my father had to talk it over with his newly-wed who was pregnant with his first daughter at that time. As I lingered in the province awaited my departure, I was getting frequent visits by my father who drove hours from the capital to see me. Every time he came he would bring alimentary provisions, with cash which was always greatly needed and appreciated. As I walked side by side with my father to his car before his left, I realized I never knew how thirsty I was to have such a presence in my life. I felt safe, I felt rich and respected. He would put hundreds of dollars in my hands, which of course my aunt always had to borrow, for which she never felt obligated to reimburse me. Great things have occurred in my life in a pattern of every five or ten years. These are occurrences that in some ways change my life profoundly, but graciously always for the better. There are factors in life that are out of our control as humans, like our destiny, or knowing the time and place and how we will die. If someone's fate could have been predicted, then many of us would have tried to cheat life and death. As I strongly believe, there's someone out there procuring stupendous deeds on my behalf, and all I have to do is belief and simply let my faith carry my heart and soul, believing that all God does He does for the best of those who trust Him, and everything will surely fall into place.

My Expatriation by My Father

By remembering that this is not an autobiography, I want to shorten my personal life's story as I create an interval from the time I actually went to live with my father in Port-au-prince and the time I came to the United States, evaluating about four years.

In succinct, during those four years I lived with my father and his wife, I had to deal with some other tough challenges with a step-mother who passionately did not want a step child around them for too long, and my presence was hindering them from creating the perfect family they were trying to establish. Thus, unlike my step-mother and their new-born daughter, and my father who have been going in and out of the United States for years as visitors, I found myself staying here in America permanently on my very first visit, with no questions asked and no explanation given to me. Imagine being left behind, abandoned in a strange country with no green card but a five-year tourist visa, on which I was allowed to stay for no longer than six months from the time I entered the United States? Well that's what happened to me, I did overstay my visit and became an illegal alien, a social condition that comes with lots of negative effects and consequences, but I had no one who cared enough to take that into consideration.

At just fifteen, I was put in a predicament which I would have to do what I had to do to dig myself out of, which was really unfair to me as a child. But I guess my father had his reasons, I just wish he talked it over with me, and made me understand why it was necessary for him to send me away so far and so fast. And maybe I wouldn't look at it in such a negative way if it came out to be that he was trying to protect me, and at the same time trying to preserve his marriage with his new family.

It was on August 1st 1990, sixteen days prior to my birthday, on which I was about to turn fifteen, when my step-mom, her three year old daughter and I boarded an airplane from Port-au-prince Haiti heading to the Unites States. We sat next to each other at the center of the airplane. Unlike many others who had gone aboard an airplane for the first time, I did not experience any motion sickness. I sat there sipping on the tiny cup of soda I was served, ate my little bag of peanut before we were served with TV dinners. We watched a movie from the small monitors placed overhead at different angles. I enjoyed flying very much, even to this day. We landed at John F. Kennedy Airport in Queens, New York. I remember as soon as we got out of the airport, my father's cousin accompanied by her husband, her mother and her two year old son were already there waiting for us. They embraced me and my little sister, and placed a quick kiss on my stepmother's cheek, for they were not on good terms with her. My baggage was put in the trunk of a different car from the one my step-mother and her daughter were supposed to depart. That very night I found myself saying goodbye to my step-mother and my little sister, and then from there we went asunder.

All along the way from the airport they were playing Haitian music that I only heard from my neighbors' house back in Haiti.

My father and his wife are Christians, and they run their house likewise by not playing or listening to those types of music in the house. But I always loved music and I was enjoying every moment of it. The roads, the sidewalks and corner stores were illuminating. I was received with opened arms, but my heart was tensed. Everything once again was unveiling right before my eyes, going through another transition, another separation.

We arrived at the apartment in Crown Heights, Brooklyn. As usual I was told to make myself at home, but as everyone knows, it is simply a metaphor which people sometime regret using after someone starts getting too comfortable in their house. So I sat down somewhere in the living room, trying to recuperate from my mental distress, I felt exhausted and nostalgic. Living with my paternal relatives whom I previously only heard of but never really get to familiarize myself with was discouraging at first, but within days I was coping fine with my new environment and surrounding. My father's cousin whom he had spoken concerning my accommodation in the United States benevolently embraced her responsibilities. She took some days off from work to help me undergo the procedures required in order to be accepted in the New York State educational systems.

On the fall of that year, I attended I.S 394-Mary McLeod Bethune Academy, located no more than eight blocks from where we lived. There I encountered many people with whom I shared my nationality fully or partially. To some I became a friend, and to others I was a true patriot, for my accent and my Haitian characteristics and my style were inevitably noticeable. In those days, the Haitians were experiencing a period of humiliation. Young Haitian-Americans who were to, kept their identity concealed, as some kept themselves secluded. Haiti was facing a political era that was unfamiliar to the Haitians and too historic to neglect by the international media, after the people of Haiti rose against the dictator regime, when President Jean Claude Duvalier was ousted and was sent into exile. As political troubles escalated, Haitian refugees were detained by bulk on the coasts of Florida on a regular basis. That created a shameful mentality within the young Haitians in the United States, which had caused them to be ashamed of who they are. There was that one kid whose name I remember to this day, but I choose to keep it discreet. At first I did not know he was Haitian, and there was no way I would have known until that day when I heard him trying to talk to a Haitian girl who was not yet as fluent in English to carry a full conversation with him, and so he was throwing some Haitian Creole here and there, for he was not fluent in Patois or French himself. From that day on we started to have little conversations, but not in the hallways of the school, nor in the cafeteria, or anywhere on school ground, because he didn't want his ethnicity to be discovered. So we rarely talk to each other, for I barely spoke or understood English myself at that time. Even after almost two decades residing in America, I still can't get rid of my accent. In fact I feel I am more explicit in writing the language than speaking it. The feeling of not being able to communicate with somebody else due to language barrier is uncomfortable, and that produces some type of sensation parallel to claustrophobia. That experience taught me how linguistic barriers could rob somebody of social advancement which has a stupendous affect on life. Someone needs to be able to communicate in order to attain achievements in such a challenging society. Whatever someone may be dealing with, without communication it's hopeless. But it wasn't too long after, things started to evolve. One by one the Haitians began to surface, the shame of being Haitian began to dissolve, and the disguises began to smear off. And that's when I realized there were many more like me in the school.

I graduated and went on to High School for Environmental Studies, a totally brand new academic institution in development at the time, when I was accepted to attend. There too, I became best friends with another student who is of Chinese origin, whom I will refer to as Benny, a pseudo name he's chosen himself, because it was easier for his non-Chinese friends to call him by. Benny and I were very much alike. The two of us were part of a small clan in the entire high school with reputable records. We were comprehensive and caring about one another's concerns. We stood up for each other in due times, we made comments about girls, who's hot and who's not, which of our teachers were nice and which ones weren't. I had nothing to reproach or reprimand him for. Every day we would take one of the trains from Columbus Circle in Manhattan, and transfer to the D train together. Then I would get off on the Parkside Avenue station, and walk to Woodruff Street where I lived for a couple of years. He would continue on toward Coney Island where he lived. He and I and his Chinese comrades became a bi-ethnic syndicate of good conducts.

One of them was a martial artist who sometime tried to teach us some moves, but unfortunately I retained nothing at all from what he has taught us, and thank God I never found myself in a situation where I would feel those karate moves would have been useful. We sat in the cafeteria together during lunch period, where we sometime witnessed other students getting abused, having their food confiscated by bullies, but they would think twice before attempting to mess with one of us. As the metaphor goes; we had each other's back.

I was the only black kid among them, and the only full blooded Haitian in the entire school for sometime, until a Haitian-American came in the picture. For that reason I was very popular, nice and humorous when I wanted to be, but rigid and serious most of the time, to the point that I was sometime mistaken for a teacher's young assistant, or a substitute teacher in training. I was also notorious for getting a lot of bad guys suspended and even expelled from school, by standing up against those who acted like the school was their turf to exercise their street behavior, preying on innocent students who didn't have a voice of their own to speak out, and without the courage to defend themselves.

I was in the gym one day with the rest of the class. A seventeen year, old six-footer, weighing over a hundred and ninety pounds, launched a basketball with such a velocity and hit an innocent girl who sat across the gym conversing and smiling with her friends. As little as I was compared to that kid, I'm only five feet and seven inches, at that time I weighed approximately a hundred and thirty pounds. It never occurred to me the size differences between me and him when I stood up and walked over as I confronted him, unveiling him as the one who threw the basketball that hit the girl. I was furious when I asked him what the hell was wrong with him. He got angry as he tried to deny it, and he picked up a chair and flung it across the floor. By then, we were set apart by deans and teachers who hasted over to restrain him as he got agitated and started to vociferate epithets. He was escorted out of the building, and was suspended for two weeks. Thereafter, he was supposed to return to the school with his parent before he could be permitted to attend classes, but he never came back. He was spotted hanging around the school on a daily basis, waiting to hang out with his friends after school. Some of his friends resented me for sometime, but eventually they came around. My conscience did reproach me for the trouble I felt to have caused, but when I remembered that innocent girl who was just sitting there, being mindful of her own affairs and talking to her friends, when abruptly her smile and contentment turned into tears and fear, I felt embolden for standing up to make him pay for what he did. Those were the consequences of what he has perpetrated, and so my remorse turned into vindictiveness.

Even now, I find myself getting upset when I see a fight on the street, infuriated when someone is getting beat up or ganged on. Although part of me wants to be all happy to enjoy life with peace of mind, trying to stay mentally and spiritually healthy by neglecting my personal worries, and ignoring negative factors around me, the greater part of me still wants to be serious and introverted, and I think those are the products of my past experiences.

In school I always felt obliged to be of such character, for my own protection and to acquire respect from my peers, especially at that particular era when Haitians had lost their respect in the eyes of the world because of past allegations. I'm really not trying to take the burden of society upon myself, but it's inevitable for me not to feel like I need to do something, when I see actions of that sort in which the small and the weak are being victimized and oppressed by the big and the strong.

My First Love

As I evolved into a young man, I have learned of factors that are imperative in my life to know about, things that have happened during my childhood that I was ignorant about, things of which I partially remembered, and things to which I am still seeking for answers. I have been traumatized by many unpleasant events in my life; events that have impacted and will affect me for a lifetime; events which had shaped me into the person that I am today. I always believed that whatever someone may become in society has so much to do with the environment, his surrounding, and most of all his personal experiences. People don't usually change by themselves even if they would want to, there must always be events or actions which provoke a reaction, which in turn cause a change within us. One of my philosophies is that people change people. People turn good into evil, we turn love into hate, angels into demons, and then we are the first to excoriate someone who is not the person he or she was once known to be. Saying she was a nice person, but she's changed, or he was in a great man, but lately he has not been himself. Well, they may not even be able to explain their new character if you questioned them on what happened, and why they are who they are now. They may not even notice the change within themselves, because it's not a change they have chosen to make, it's something that simply occurs naturally.

I have been molded into this person that I am, incapable of trusting anyone, not even family members. When I think of my life, how frustrating and distressful I get sometime, I would ask God why or why me? These questions remain out there unanswered. But recently I began to understand that everything happens in someone's life for a specific purpose, even when one may not fully comprehend what the purpose is, but eventually the purpose will be revealed.

Despite all the personal dilemmas I've encountered, what annoys me the most is the strong affection I am filled with for my homeland. It marvels me to the point of asking myself, how can a young man living in America, where is said to be the land of opportunity, where anyone has the chance to bring dreams to reality, I find myself worrying about how to create a better life for my people?

Why can't I find the ego within like everyone else, to pursue my own personal goals and privileges?

I find myself lost in my own world, though I am physically here due to circumstances transcending back home, my spirit, my mind and my heart remain in Haiti. My thoughts and my prayers, my pleas and my intercessions are all on behalf of my people and my land. All I envision is for Haiti to either take a giant step backward to the way it once was, or to advance technologically, industrially, politically, to advance to be a civilized nation like any other advanced society in the world.

Why can't I be more introverted about my well being, the well being of my family and my future like most people?

I take upon my shoulders the burden of every Haitian, feeling more remorseful than those who have actually harmed them, and bringing the country to its decadence. I have tried forcefully to fight my feelings, trying to stop caring so much, by placing all the blames on the men who should be held accountable for creating the cruel conditions that my people are in, but to no avail. I believe some of our past leaders did not try hard enough, I feel some of them did not try at all, but instead those sentiments keep causing me to be vindictive about the whole circumstance, which always drag me deeper into the situation I tried to evade.

Although it is true they are responsible, I sought in my heart to forgive them, because revenge is not the answer, revenge is not love, but revenge is vendetta, which is precisely what have been going on for decades in Haiti, between political parties and their supporters with different views of others.

Rev. Martin Luther King Jr. had a dream, but I have a vision. I envision that one day Haiti will reclaim its title as The Pearl of the Caribbean, or should we then call it something more exotic like The Paradise Under the Sun? Which would sound beautifully in French, La Paradie Sous Le Ciel! A place where the people will no longer live by chances and risks, but they will face their daily life with certitude that the next day their children will not die of starvation and malnutrition, or of any diseases that are curable but unreachable due to lack of money or scarceness of doctors and nurses.

They will not grow up to be indigents like our forefathers, but they will live to be great men and women, sons and daughters who will make parents proud. They will live to witness the future as they carry the ethos of the Haitian nation through generations to come.

The day will eventually come when my people will once again be emancipated. This time not from the French or any other super power of the world, but from their political predicament, which has been leading to economic cataclysm, to social malaise, causing mental distress even in the mind of our innocent children.

I'm saying this with power and authority, that I will not die before, during, or after I witness another revolution in Haiti. I will live for that glorious day, I will witness it, I will rejoice in it with every breath I will take, along with my fellow patriots, young and old, we will harmoniously sing of our deliberation from poverty, from economic destabilization, from misanthropes who wish to see us falter, who are latently conspiring to see us crumble in desperation on our quest for a better Haiti, after two hundred years of independence.

We will not beg for bread, we will not dishonor ourselves before any man; we do not need their sympathy. Let the hypocrites stand by and be sightseers and spectators to great courage, as we regain our strength from our misfortune, and rise up before their eyes to victory once again. And the best part of all this is that no one will be able to do a damn thing about it. Their obstructions will be in vain, their diplomacy against us shall be futile, and their arrows shall be diverted into their own hearts. Then they will have no choice but to be convinced about whom we are, to recognize and become admissive to our greatness, our courage and our values.

Politics and Society

I am a child of the late seventies generation, and the first government of which I scarcely know anything about was the Duvalier regime. What I can remember by far is that, from the time I began to have some knowledge of certain things, until the time that I came to the United States, I was always fascinated with the governmental systems, the power of one man, the patriotic activities, the mobilization of the population, cleaning, washing out and decorating the streets for presidential convoy, even when the president's motorcade is just passing through for a visit to another town.

Very frequently the men of the Armed Forces of Haiti known as the Leopards, would circulate the streets of Petion-Ville, a suburb in the capital city where I lived from my childhood. Those men were always looking spruce in their military uniform. Their helmet, their dark shades, ammo belt around their waist, their black and shiny boots on the feet, on their back or in hands were M-16s and a revolver on their side, standing fierce with the aspect of rigidity on their face, as they drive by on military trucks parading the suburbs. We had a cleaner environment, our people were more courteous, and children were more respectful and respectable. From the capital city to the far regions of the provinces, everyone managed to survive and live comfortably, regardless of their trade, skills or profession. Our livestock were bred naturally to be delectable and nutritious. Our fruits were succulent, and our vegetables were fresh. Along with so much more that made life in Haiti beautiful and envied, especially by people who visited the paradise country on occasional basis.

Haiti certainly deserved the love it received from its people and visitors and migrants who fell in love with it and its culture. Therefore if the Duvalier regime was a syndicate of villains and corruptors as some people have claimed it to be, then I think I was too young to know or understand it. There is absolutely nothing I can say to denigrate the Duvalier dynasty, nor can I say anything to justify any of their misconducts. However, my concern is what is going on in the country today. Freedom of speech may be limited in some societies, but in some intense cases some people can't help it but to speak their minds when it comes to factors that affect them, their family, or their country. Only an idiot and a coward would stand by with arms crossed, stagnant and speechless, while witnessing his family becoming victims of someone else's ignorant actions. Only a fool would continue to say he is not involved in politics and remain oblivious to political activities. A nation under any government is affected by every move or decision taken by that government. Whether anyone wants to be part of it or not, it is impossible to abstain from the political world. The children have to go to school, businesses have to operate, everything has to be regulated, and laws have to be enforced for the protection of every citizen and resident of that society. When students can no longer speak their minds, journalists are disappearing without a trace for their bodies to be found, when people can't afford to support themselves and their loved ones, when someone gets viciously hurt on the verge of dying by the hands of government officials, then when the victim arrives at the hospital there is either no doctors nor proper equipments or medicines to care for him, then they become incontrovertible concerns. When the citizens of a country rather have their life risked at sea with the hope of finding a better life on estrange lands, it is no longer just politics, it becomes a personal matter, a patriotic factor, a civil and global concern.

I can't enumerate how many times I have watched on television hundreds of Haitian refugees being apprehended from the coast of Florida, and they are sent back to precisely where and what they were optimistically trying to escape. They precariously do it over and over again, even when they know what the outcome would be. In their mind they say it doesn't hurt to try, they rather try to escape hell on earth from Haiti, then to stay in such a turmoil and discouraging environment. They just won't die with the remorse of not trying to save their children or themselves. Whenever I watch those events being broadcasted via the television, I always ask why I have to witness it, because it's always a heartbroken broadcast to see, a sad story hear, how my people are being treated like vagrants at the hands of strangers who in fact are ethically challenged themselves. Then again realizing that they are not getting a better treatment at home forced me to sympathize with them. In fact they are being treated in worse manners by their own people on their own turf. They're being exploited, battered, murdered, humiliated. Those who die of starvation, those who continue to live with scars of injustice, those who are dismembered, all at the hands of those they trusted the most, the ones who they perceived as brothers, the ones who are positioned to protect them from their enemies. Where there is deceit trust vanishes, where there is misguidance there is no more faith, where there is hatred love succumbs, where love and unity are absent there is nothing left but destruction.

As the optimist that I am, I still believe there is hope for the Haitian people. I still believe that Haitians can and will regain their strength, and Haiti will stand as the pillar of the Caribbean once more. I am still hopeful that things will get better. The regime that is leading it to failure will crumble, but the people of Haiti will triumph to victory from the hands of their oppressors. The irony is that, the president who should be managing his position in justice is doing the exact opposite, as the majority of the people remain a multitude of fanatics who seem to be incoherent about what's going on, meanwhile they are manifesting the glory of a decimator, the man known as Jean Bertrand Aristide.

A SCOUNDREL IN CHARGE

This book was primarily intended to penetrate the minds of the Haitian population, in efforts to bring an end to the Lavalas regime, but fortunately for all of us, that purpose was defeated on February the 29th of 2004. Therefore at this point, everything you will read pertaining to Jean Bertrand Aristide may seem like current events, although it's been five years since he had left the country. For this book has been in process while he was actually in power. I think that way you can feel what I felt when I was hitting the keys on my computer keyboard bringing this project into perspective.

Here is a timeline of Jean Bertrand Aristide's presidency, on which the following paragraphs are based:

7 February1991- 30 September1991; Seated
15 June 1993-12 May1994; Exiled
12 October 1994-7 February 1996; Seated
7 February 2001-29 February 2004; Seated

So much has gone terribly wrong during the Lavalas reign in Haiti. The people are just a time bomb waiting to explode, while their president is a latent, virulent viper waiting to be manifested abroad daylight. Many of those who are loyal fanatics and believers of him will realize they were in an incubus state for all those years. By then it will be too late for many of them who are extremely insane about this regime, that they are determined even to put their heads on a guillotine for their president. I'm not against loyalty, for that is a proof of trust and love, but my question is, is he loyal to them as they are loyal to him? And according to what my eyes have seen and what my ears have heard, he is certainly not returning the favor of being a loyal president to those who entrust him with their life and the country.

Now I realize the reason for which he came in the character of a Good Samaritan, a benevolent and a philanthropist, pretending to be for the poor and the illiterates, and not for the upper class and the bourgeoisie. Due to the simple fact that the mass of the population is in destitution, and illiteracy is overwhelming, he figured that their ignorance of the political movements will in fact get him elected. He gets to fool them by his gibberish in his so-called speeches, using parabolic expressions to communicate to those who most of the times don't even understand the words that come out of his mouth. He gets away with it and acquires fame and popularity. But the limited percentage of over eight million people living in Haiti, who have worked hard to attain their baccalaureates, those who are doctors in philosophy and theology, and intellectuals, some of whom have studied abroad, the ones who also run the economy, they can't be deceived or misled, for they know that Aristide is a snake who has disguised himself in sheepskin to baffle innocent vulnerable individuals, and that most of his statements are paradox.

Using reverse psychology and sarcasm in his euphoric speeches, he turns the poor against the wealthy, the ugly against the lovely, that way he could remain their sole attraction, to be perceived as the savior of the mass population. Meanwhile the economy is in critical state, the cost of living is skyrocketing. Most investors are taking their businesses elsewhere, those who have sold their properties and settled themselves and their families abroad, while he remains the national leach, sucking up the blood and the strength of the Haitian people, smuggling the resources of the country into his own pockets. All those factors contribute to the isolation of my people and the regression of my country.

Some people just can't admit their incapability to procure and achieve positive goals and dreams, and by them challenging their personal incompetence with inferiority, they drag innocent ones with them, oblivious to the fact that they are being responsible for not only their own soul, but the lives and souls of others as well. If Aristide was not such a selfish arrogant man, then he would not have tried to return to Haiti and get reinstated on power in 1994. If he indeed cared about the well-being of his own people, he would have been conscious of his inabilities to restore the better life that the Haitian people are in need of. He would have ceded his position to someone else who is sincere at heart, someone who is a true man by admitting to his faults and incompetence, someone who is not in denial that his strength and abilities cannot surpass certain heights and boundaries, someone who doesn't try to go beyond his strength while causing other people to suffer, someone who is indeed capable of doing the job.

No one is perfect, that too I know, and therefore I don't believe anyone can handle particularly the situations of Haiti impeccably. However if the comprehension and the love of a person with the love of the patriots for our country are mutual, then it would have been manifested in one way or another in a positive light, just like the wickedness in Aristide has been manifested in obscurity. As bad as things have gotten, I really don't see anything he could come up with now that would propitiate the pain and the anger he had caused to the Haitian people.

Jean Bertrand Aristide adopted the word Lavalas as an emblem under which his political party floats, but what the word Lavalas means in our linguistic definition and comprehension says it all.

In our society and in our language, Lavalas is a slang word utilized mainly by peasants and illiterates, people who may have never entered a classroom once in their life. They express themselves in their own ways. They develop their own skills of communication, which they adapt themselves to. Their children grow up listening to that language and learning it by natural instinct. Between those who migrate from the rural regions into another, and the erudite travelers who often visit those places, who are obligated to communicate at their own exploitation, before one knows it a large portion of the population is already disseminated with that type of language. Our country is constituted of two official languages, the French, and the Haitian Patois which is a derivation of the French. The word Lavalas as far as I know, simply means inundation, flood, or deluge.   It is an informal term which cannot even be utilized in the classrooms to instruct our children. Like in every other civilized nation, in Haiti too we find a certain groups of people who choose to express themselves using terms that are in contrast to the official languages.

In the event of an inundation, streams of water are condensed from every angle to create a watercourse through the rural districts, taking along everything in its path, from debris to agricultural resources. But depending on the intensity and its velocity, a flood may cause major geographical damages; it may destroy lives of animals, damage homes, and even destroy human lives. A flood is always filthy, impure, destructive and dangerous. Therefore according to the description I just gave of the word Lavalas, it could be easily grasped that there are two sides to its meaning. One side of it could be interpreted as a process of purification, in which the flood purges the region of its debris. The other side is, especially on an island like Haiti that has very few drainage or sewer systems, a flood simply means destruction. During the reign of the Lavalas regime, recapitulating on the events that took place in Haiti, I began to realize why an intellectual person and a savvy like Aristide would choose such a word to represent his political party. What I thought about him from the beginning is a fact. When he chose to entitle his political party Lavalas, he knew precisely what he was doing, he knew why he chose it, and what he meant by it. Aristide is not an idiotic man who speaks vaguely and carelessly. He is an intelligent, experienced priest who chooses his words very carefully, who pronounces them with projection and articulation. Those who have the skills to comprehend they understand, and those who don't possess the ears to hear and the spirit to discern they perished. Everyone who is conscious of what's going on in Haiti would concur that he is indeed what his party stands for in the flesh as in the spirit. He has been operating in adherence to what he has constituted, as to what the word Lavalas is construed, which I personally interpret to be genocide.

When the people of Haiti finally emerge from obscurity, awaken from their dormant state, and realize that Aristide is a manipulative person, with a self-indulging character, a scoundrel who managed to penetrate and command the spirit of his acolytes, who has exploited the weakness of a starving nation, it will be too late. When they finally realize how he had deceived so many innocent people who are educationally paralyzed, targeted them by using metaphorical expressions to acquire fame and wealth, to satisfy his arrogant desires, it will be hell to pay, and I will not feel a bit of sympathy for him. I'm just hoping that this time the people will be more astute on the subject to not allow him the privilege the others had, to go abroad and enrich other nations, living luxuriously on the millions he has stolen from the Haitian people. That's why the majority of the population has nothing to survive on, and nothing to depend on, because all their wealth have been compiled into the pockets of those they have sent into exile.

Trust Is Virulent

Most people think of an enemy as someone whom they have had arguments with at some point in time, who have shown or declared enmity toward them. Some people look out to protect themselves when they are around complete strangers or rivals. Some think an enemy is someone who has personally expressed or exhibited extreme resentment toward them, their beliefs or their practices. But what they all fail to realize is that the enemy may be none of those I have just described, but someone who is trustworthy, someone they know, someone who lives, eats and drinks with them, even someone whom they sleep on the same bed with. An enemy could be the one you share your thoughts with, the one who knows everything about you from the color of your eyes to the core of your heart. Someone who's relationship with you is cohesive. Those are the type of enemies who are most dangerous and virulent of them all. They don't have to go far or make any real efforts to swallow their prey, since they have the access that a complete stranger or an obvious enemy wouldn't have to get close to their potential victims. Not only such enemies are latent and lethal, pretending to be best friends of yours, but they could also be biological or lawful relatives of yours, which makes situations much more complex to control and deal with, because relatives cannot be easily evaded, nor can they really be perceived as enemies. Regardless of what may occur between two family members, when they look deeply into their heart, there is a little sediment of love and attachment between them which no one and nothing can ever take away even after death. However don't be naïve, it's surprising what one could do to the other. They worm around you like saints, with kindness and care, gaining your trust, study your actions, regulate your arrival and your departure, your strength and your weakness, so that the coup and the snare they have prepared for you could be intelligently, efficiently and effectively executed. They are the ones who would cut your throat and not even think twice about it, and they would have no remorse at all about what they have done, because they have had enough time to think about it. They study the possibilities thoroughly, they ruminate over whatever is it they hate about you, and when they are ready to execute their premeditated act, they go at full force and leave no place for regrets. Believe it or not, we are surrounded by those typical individuals in our society, in our institutions, in our respective homes, even in the most ironic places like our church, where it may even be the ones you show reverence to within a congregation. Therefore how divine can a politician be, not to expect characteristics of that sort from him, regardless of his religion or beliefs? On the contrary, most politicians have no friends, all they care about is their popularity, telling you what they know you want to hear to exploit your vote and secure their position. Aristide is that type of man, a latent enemy to the Haitian people, sooner or later everything he is will come to light, when everyone will see how artificial and wicked he is, and as the Haitian metaphor goes, jou sa pa-p gin dlo k-pou lave-l, meaning nothing will justify him.

He presented himself as a democratic citizen of Haiti, proclaiming to restore Democracy, gaining exterior supports from other democratic forces in the world as well as interior supports from the majority of the people in the country. He misled his fanatics into voting him to power, and once he was there, he prove to everyone the type of beast he really is, a hoaxer who made a farce out of many, who brought denigration upon himself, and who may still seeking for the true definition of the word Democracy in his vocabulary. Meanwhile he's leading the people by his own interpretation of the word, which is far from what he believes it to be.

It's All about the People

What is Democracy?

The definition of the word Democracy may vary from one dictionary and another. However it is prevalently understood by most people to mean simply the people, by the people, for the people, with the people, and about the people, which is what all governments should be about. Democracy is definitely not an emblem under which neither citizens nor government officials are ordained to exercise their personal desires. It does not give anyone the permission to murder, to covet, to exploit, to seek personal indulgence, and certainly not to commit injustice or to yield the right to immorality.

Now-a-days we find men and women who have been caught in the leadership syndrome, utilizing Democracy as a way to confound people into getting them to office, but their deeds contradict their promises, leaving people wondering if they really knew what that word is. They speak against Dictatorship, Totalitarianism, and Imperialism. In Haiti we hear some of them excoriate Duvalierism, but they too, once in the position of power, they end up practicing the same methods of governing, with the same systematic agendas. Their actions could be defined as the worse ever experienced from previous governments, except that they do it under the emblem of

Democracy unlike the Duvalier regime, known to have been a dictatorship.

Democracy does not fabricate enmity; it does not disunite a nation, turning neighbors and relatives against one another, the poor against the wealthy, the paralytic against the valiant, and tenants against proprietors. Democracy does not grant anyone the right under any government to go around raping young girls while forcing their parents to watch, or raping a mother as her children are bound to chairs, with guns pointed right at their temple, witnessing such a heinous act. Fathers are being shot in front of their wife and children. I even heard of an incident where a son was forced into having sexual intercourse with his own mother. That is a disgrace, an abomination in the eyes of all men and God, even in the eyes of the most ignorant, sick minded and twisted individual upon the face of this planet. Those are things some have heard and others have optically witnessed under the Lavalas regime. Thoughts and actions normal people would think could only be cogitated in the mind of a wicked individual, who can only be coerced by some type of satanic spirit to commit. But those actions were executed by armed government officials whose jobs are to protect the citizens of a country from being victims of any type of malice, leaving them behind to live and cope with the humiliation and the excruciating memories.

When the people of a district or a state choose a person to represent them in public affairs, and the president himself sat in conclave with his political subjects, disregarding constitutional provisions and pre-selects his personal friend to occupy that same position prior to Election Day, that is not Democracy.

It is purely nepotism, it's unethical and immoral, it is a contradiction to what Aristide said he came to establish. This is neither hearsay nor a fabrication, it is a factual development I personally witnessed during an election in Haiti in 1995, and it was my very own father and his supporters who were victims of that injustice.

My father has been serving his community alongside his father since he was twenty-one years old. After his father retired from the Public Organization, EPPLS, my father remained there, pursued his education and obtained a degree in Accounting. EPPLS in French stands for, Enterprise Publique de Promotion de Logements Sociaux, meaning Public Enterprise for Promoting Social Housing. The main function of that Enterprise is to assist people around the country, who are striving to survive below the poverty line, with affordable housing. Those people are also facilitated with other essential elements such as water and electricity. As anyone who knows my father could testify, he is a wonderful person at heart and also in character. He is a philanthropist, a man who would go to the extreme to make sure someone else has a place to stay, food to eat, and most of all, making certain that every child he encounters has a chance to get some type of education. He makes sure that every young adult he knows acquire at least some vocational courses. As long as he sees the determination for learning in someone, he will make it a burden to lend a hand so that person could make something out of himself in society.

My father has a syndrome for learning. He's always seeking for information, always attending classes, taking courses after work, and still manages to keep control of his family affairs and everything else. My father's name fits his character perfectly, he is a true Guerrier. Out of his own pockets, he would dispense to pay rent for some who are less fortunate than most. There is a metaphor in the Haitian culture that says, "what the right hand does is no business of the left"; that has been proven to be also my father's philosophy. He has spent so much of his own money to help other people; his wife would tell me she doesn't know what he does with his money. Everything he's worked for cannot be accounted for. His savings account has been depleted, and no one would know about the financial assistance he's given to people. He does not complain, as he remains a benefactor to many with the little bit he has. As time passed, we began to uncover the good deeds my father has sown, not just in his community, but in other regions around the country. With such a character and his position in the public eyes, my father became a well-known public servant and a respectable personality to many, a father figure to the fatherless, a good friend to despairing mothers, as his popularity grew undeniably large and incontestably strong.

My father admits it all the time that it wasn't his idea or his love for politics that led him to run for mayor in 1995. Everyone knows that politics in general is a very dangerous ground to walk, and a stressful career to pursue, whether it is in America or in a small tribal village in the far end of Africa. A politician always has to have a sixth sense, he has to have the spirit of discernment, he needs eyes in the back of the head, and he always has to sleep with one eye open as he takes intermittent naps at night. True politicians have hard time sleeping in their beds, they are always too busy meditating and thinking about how to improve certain conditions that their country and their people are dealing with. Imagine how much difficult and heart wrenching it is to be a politician in a place like Haiti, where the conditions are far more deplorable. It will take more than just money and great efforts, and a man of a good heart and good will, to improve our land and our conditions. It takes bloodshed in some cases to assure that some criminal activities don't occur in the future. My father never anticipated on taking part in politics. But those who know him and his deeds in the communities he serves proposed the idea to him to run for public office. They knew his strength, they believed in him, and they were his arms and legs supporting him throughout his campaign. They believed that such position would broaden his capability and possibility to do what he loves, to do what he does best, which is helping people, becoming a voice apparatus in places where the murmurs of the people are not respected.

During the course of my father's campaign, we experienced some difficult moments which had proven that Democracy was far from reaching the land of Haiti. We didn't mean to be naïve or to leave any room for deceit and disappointments; we knew there has never been a Democratic Government in Haiti from the beginning of time. However since Aristide presented himself as a Democratic president, we skeptically expected him to prove it by letting candidates outside his party have a fair chance at serving the people and their community, but what we got was not what we know a Democratic Election should be.

My father had a couple of banners mounted in two locations in his campaigning district, advertising his candidacy. On a Saturday morning my father received a phone call from a supporter who wanted to know if he had ordered the banners to be taken down, and of course the answer was no. When we rushed to the locations consecutively, both of them were cut down and confiscated; only the strings that held them up were hanging from the light poles from which they were fastened. From that moment, we knew that we were definitely in for a political battle, but we didn't know how it was going to be fought and how it would end.

Election Day came, all of our supporters did their due diligence to go out and vote, my father was confidently undefeated. There was absolutely no one deserving, no one popular enough to stand against my father in that election. In fact he won that election by a landslide which we all had anticipated. But on the day of the results, supporters gathered around their audio receptors waiting to hear the good news, while at home our family and friends were in the same position, but in a different mindset, for we had the information that others didn't have. A friend of the family who is also my father's godfather by marriage, worked for the government. He had told my father that someone had already been officially chosen by President Aristide to be the mayor of that same district. Effectively, the results came out, everything my father was told was true. I was inconsolably enraged. The women were distraught and weeping hysterically. But in the midst of all, something caught my attention, and it was the way my father reacted to the situation maturely and composed. He found the courage to embolden us and the others by saying, "In a battle there must be a winner which makes the opponent the loser, we have ran a great campaign and fought a hard battle, and therefore we have nothing to blame or reproach ourselves for, we have given our all in this fight, our failure is not because we are weak but it is a product of injustice." I thought those were the most sincere words coming out of a man who had just been victimized by the arrogance of another, in a country and a community he has spent years serving and sweating for, in an effort to improve their life conditions. Although I was intrigued by my father's response to the situation, although I have great respect for him, and that I support him in what he stands for and all, but there is this question I always ask myself, can I ever be like him? Thus I realized that I really don't want to be like my father after all. I don't want to be a sheep; I want to be a lion. I don't want to turn the other cheek; I want to strike back and destroy my enemy. As the oldest son who just turned nineteen when I was in Haiti for the election, I felt vindictive toward Aristide and his regime, but I was not in the position to act upon it. I was a novice in many fields, and it hurt me profoundly that I was unable to help my father during that rough and disappointing moment of our life.

Now here I am many years after, Aristide has been ousted and reinstated, he is now in exile in the Central African Republic, and still he's one person whose spirit and mine are never at peace. If I say that hatred was never part of my feelings for Aristide then I would be in denial, and I have no reason at all to deny that, for I am afraid of no one but my own immoral deeds in the eyes of God, and my conscience that judges me. I am a man with a heart, and my destiny is not even in my own hands but hidden and protected in God. However, during the course of time I became spiritually mature, I began to perceive life differently in a person, which has attributed to my comprehension of people's ignorance and mishaps as well as their ways and styles of life. But that does not mean I have to accept and endure the pain that somebody is causing me, or my family, or in this case my country and my people.

My intension is not to incriminate Aristide as a process to upright myself for political ambitions, but I feel it's my duty as a Haitian progeny to stand up for my country in any circumstance, to pull up my trousers and my sleeves, to battle injustice, to combat immorality, to speak against genocide, or any other factors that may be hindrances between my people and prosperity. What makes matters worse, is when so many people are suffocating from the situations that have made their lives unbearable, and they are afraid of speaking out and showing their frustration, afraid that they will be retaliated against. The Haitian people are being tortured physically, mentally, psychologically, which definitely affect their spirituality and their self-esteem. For that reason I decided to take a stand, to become a vessel for those who are speaking through me, to exhale and release the excruciating sentiments they have kept for so long in their feeble heart.

I am compelled to speculate on this, like my aunt usually told me when I did something she disagreed upon; I do not hate Aristide, like I shouldn't hate any human being, but I hate his character, I resent what he stands for, and I extremely disappointed in him for what he has done to Haiti and my people. After a long era in bondage under the Duvalier regime, how that government was such a tyranny according to many, this is not what the people of Haiti anticipated when they elected a man who presented himself as a follower of the Divine Scriptures, as a people person. They expected someone who should have been the man of his words, a man of integrity, and a man whose deeds are the fruits of his swell character, someone who should have been an arm in the emancipation of the Haitian people from their relentless sufferings. But those characters are exactly what we cannot use to describe Aristide, whom the Haitian people have given power over their lives, and not one of his followers is protected from his wrath.

During his time on power, the country has been brought to its lowest degradation unlike none the most ancient one in Haiti has ever seen or known before. Excoriating someone is one thing, despising what someone does is one thing, rejecting his friendship because of ethical, cultural, religious or social differences is one, feeling unforgiving toward someone is one, but as a human being no one should feel spiteful toward another, for life is a gift naturally and rightfully given to everyone and everything that breathes. No one under the sky is permitted under any rights whatsoever to deprive someone else of his naturally given life, or to feel someone deserves to be put to death regardless of his wrongdoings. If someone does feel that way about someone else, then I should say that person indeed is the one who should not be part of the human race. For anyone with such a thought is considered inhuman himself, and a statement of that sort cannot be justified under any circumstances. But if I say that, it would be a contradiction of my own belief, which would make me no better than a liar and a misanthrope myself. Although I believe no man should be punished by death at the hands of other men, I believe every man should be punished for their crimes accordingly. Aristide should be trialed and charged according to the crimes he's committed during his reign as the president of Haiti. He ought to be held accountable for the deaths of innocent people, journalists, businessmen, hard working class citizens who opposed him. Those who have been kidnapped directly or indirectly by his followers, those who have been brainwashed by his words and theories to go out and create confusion, while he retained his position, watching all those crimes unfolding and did absolutely nothing to stop them.

INEQUALITY IN SOCIETY

Histories have been documented, archived, and published about the hardship that different groups of people had suffered in the early civilizations in of world. When I study about ancient civilizations such as the Greeks, the Romans, and the Egyptians, I came across some very significant data. In Greece, we learn how the women were treated differently from the women in Athens, with very little or no right at all in society. However the women in Sparta were treated in much better ways, with the women being the dominant figures in the households. In Rome, women were considered to be child-bearers and possessions, they had no identity, they were not given individual names, they were not thought to be worthy of individuality. A baby girl was only given the middle name of the father, or nomen, to indicate which social class or family she belonged to. This is a very small part of the great inequality and discriminatory status that existed in the ancient civilizations.

Slavery has played a major role in every great society, as we know that's one of the reasons they have become the great civilizations and empires they once were. In Egypt, the Israelites were kept hostage and enslaved under King Pharaoh, because they were viewed as inferiors by the Egyptians. It has been in discussion between scholars about how many years the Israelites were in Egypt. Some say they were in slavery between four hundred to four hundred and thirty years, but most scholars have concluded in enumerating that duration by four generations instead. Therefore for four generations, or if we choose to say over four hundred years, the Israelites were in slavery. They bore children in the sludge, laboring from dawn till dusk for no type of salary, as they were whipped when they became weary under the bright scorching sun. From my exegesis, extrapolating from different sources, about six hundred thousand strong men walked out of Egypt. And after including women and children, the amount exceeds over two and a half million Israelites who actually crossed the red sea, with Moses as their liberator and faithful leader. Although thousands of them died after spending forty years in the wilderness for disobedience and misconduct, the Israelites did enter the promise land but without Moses, who was forbidden to enter it, also for disobedience. I'm not questioning God, I am not in the position to even consider doing something like that, but I feel that it was a cruel and unusual punishment after all Moses had done. But God is all powerful and does what He pleases, besides, in this time and age I'm not going to spend my time worrying and feeling sympathetic about Moses, I have my own case to plea. Moses died and his body was never found. But I'm certain he's in a better place, for God is not unjust to neglect or forget the good deeds of anyone, whether it is mine, yours, and certainly not those of Moses, a man who was closer to God than any of us could ever be.

That same treatment was repeated further down the line, when black people were traded on a national scale as properties by and to white slave owners. Like the Israelites in Egypt, black people were also mistreated, but the difference was that they didn't have a name, and their identity was simply their complexions which determined their intrinsic values, which led their destiny.

Discrimination and racism never cease to exist among us even after so many centuries. As a matter of fact things have taken turn for the worse over the years. Racism to me is the unethical form of crime that exists in our societies, it is simply not recognized to be a crime punishable by law like any other crimes, because it's really a feeling, and unless it is acted upon verbally or physically it remains oblivious and virtually inexistent. However I feel that racial behaviors should be treated punishably as any other crime. Racism is still globally alive within our civilizations in a way that seems to be acceptable because people don't have the eyes to see it, or they do see it but try to neglect it, overlooking that racial crimes are still being committed with no actions taken against them. We don't even need to do profound research to realize that most of our black nations are always experiencing tough conditions. They are always in predicaments caused by suppressions from some powerful government that tries to control everything. They control the economy; they control governments of small countries by creating turmoil and instigating civil wars among them. They even control the air space by instituting no fly zone restrictions, keeping others from flying above their lands, meanwhile trying to take over other planets in outer space. Like the Haitians, many black nations are oppressed by economic and political instability, causing frustrations among the people who turn against each other, which directly put us in a situation where we feel obliged to migrate to other countries in such of a better life. Most of the time we end up in a country where the population is predominantly Caucasian, who treat us with inferiority, as we exuberate their economy by performing duties they would never perform themselves, for lower wages and in worse conditions.

There are so many questions to be answered, like why is South Africa dealing with apartheid? Why are most of the African nations dying from diseases that are curable but treatments are limited due to financial situation or other reasons? In Haiti when we hear about the upper class citizens, they are usually the mulattoes and other Caucasian immigrants who just love the tropical lifestyle away from the frigid winter climate in their own country. They are the ones who build and reside on the oceanfront, with beautiful yachts on their beaches, living lavishly, while the indigenous children of the country continue to live in poverty. Some of them never get to feel, or enjoy, or love, or know what the country actually means to them until they travel abroad, and that's when they realize what they have which they never care to protect and love. The children of Africa, the greatest continent on earth, the source of the origin of mankind are fighting every day to survive relentless famine, and other deplorable conditions. That is not natural, that's not the way it's supposed to be, and someway somehow our forefathers' slave owners have something to do with it. The black nations are falling deeper into regression, particularly the independent ones. The only black nations that are doing a little better economically are those under the occupation of one of the so-called greater powers, governed by Caucasians, and we all know those greater powers don't give a penny unless they get triple of that amount in return one way or another, even if they have to shed blood for it. It is shameful but true, that some people choose to trade their freedom for rice, and canned beans, and turkey wings. I am not here to judge, and I understand it's their freedom and therefore have the right to do whatever they want with it, but it's baffling to me.

Right here in America, after numerous campaigns that have been conducted to eliminate discrimination and racism, hatred is so deep within the heart of some people that it's become a sickness that's impossible to be completely extirpated. We still find on both parts, black and white families who don't believe in miscegenation, although sometime the chemistry between miscegenational couples could produce very beautiful offspring.

I believe that there are unique individuals put on earth to fulfill specific purposes. It's not ironic that I am here proofreading and making amendments to this project which I started many years ago as I witness Barack Obama living in the White House with his family as the First African American president of the United States. He is undeniably a perfect product of miscegenational chemistry. President Barack Obama's success to this point in the American history has shifted everybody's perceptions to a better understanding that racial barriers can be broken, like any other barriers which may stand between a man and his dreams. I am inclined to believe that Mr. Obama was predestined to be who he is today, for histories as such can only be dreamt of and not made possible by men, it takes divine powers to realize a dream so stupendous. People all over the world, particularly the Americans can now view society from different lenses, which will hopefully lead to a better America for future generations. Likewise, I believe there is a man out there who will one day find the courage to face the challenges that are being confronted by the Haitian people. That man will be the one to save Haiti from its predicaments. However, there are major purges to be done, major changes to be made on educating the people on many factors that concern them and their country. Factors such as how to manage the natural and constructive resources on our homeland, how to stay united in the midst of all circumstances, working together to find solutions for our own problems, laboring in perfect harmony for a remedy to cure our own national illnesses.

We have made so many mistakes in the past, electing the wrong candidates, giving our hearts to candidates who are only about themselves and not about the people and the country. I have personally witnessed demonstrators who have been revolting against past regimes by burning down national monuments, by torching residences of politicians who have been forced into exile. Many citizens, some of whom had been politically involved, those who had been regular working class citizens, had been forced out of the country with their immediate family, had their properties vandalized, and their lands taken over by vagabonds, with a mere chance of ever set foot on their homeland again. I personally feel resentful of that misconception, and the Haitian people need to learn to deal and master their anger differently and intelligently. The government as well has to learn how to approach a frustrating people without provoking them, particularly a people who had been deceived and exploited, a people in despair, a nation that is desperately in need of food and shelter, and other essentials to survive in a challenging society. Someone's outpouring anger is the expression of dissatisfaction, which most of the time is too overwhelming to contain. I believe that people of any country should be granted freedom of speech, and when they speak out their pain and suffering, when they show their discontentment to a government, they should be able to do it without fear, without having to suffer hardship from the authorities or anyone else, as long as they do it peacefully in order and discipline.

I believe members of the Haitian government, who are naturally part of our nation, are also part of our land, and they too should be protected by the constitution like every other citizen of the country. People do have the propensity to exaggerate, which leads them to the extent of the law, nevertheless the law should not consist of any clause that force a natural born citizen to expatriate his country, have his properties destroyed, nor should he or any relatives of his be persecuted. The law is there to prosecute violators of the constitution, and therefore if anyone in the government commits a crime, the law is there to prosecute him just like anyone else. If a member of the government or the president himself is arraigned and found guilty of a crime, then let him be incarcerated and punished according to his sentence. But whatever that person has worked for and procured successfully should be left intact for the use of his wife and children. If in any case, his wife and children had voluntarily left or decided to flee the country for whatever their personal reasons may be, then let his residence be utilized as an orphanage, a military post, or any other purposes that would be useful to the community. As for the demolition of constructive assets simply because a certain individual owned it, or the expatriation of a Haitian born citizen with all the money he has pocketed from the national treasury while on power, is certainly not a wise idea, it is unbeneficial to the country, and it is ethically incorrect. One of the former presidents, Jean Claude Duvalier, who had succeeded his father during the Duvalier dynasty from 1957-1986, probably and most likely had many properties and other assets in their possession, and money that was more than enough to be spent toward the country's infrastructures. Now expatriating a man like that to enjoy life as he dispenses all the capital that has been collected between him and his father's reign, as he boosts up the economy of another nation was purely idiotic. This man along with his money should have been in Haiti, either incarcerated or else, but we know for sure that the money he's pocketed would have been put to good use for the benefits of the nation.

It's What's Best for My People

Some people may find hostility in the manner I speak of Aristide. But I anticipated that, and it's very simple to explain. He's done nothing better than the former presidents we've had. As a matter of fact he's probably the worse we've ever known, juxtaposed to the previous ones during whose regimes we had experienced a country of respect, a nation of pride, and a land envied by tourists who travel from around the world to indulge in our cultural values.

He has been inculpated in bringing the country into the ditch it's been for decades, which has deepen over the years he has been on power. My people are not in need of someone like Aristide to rob them of the little bit they have. We don't need someone who comes up from the bottom of the social class, who pretends to understand the misery the nation is facing so he could get to where he wants to be, or someone who indeed understands nothing at all about the hunger of the people and how to provide for them. Someone who already has his own doesn't necessarily go after someone else's by force unless he is saturated with greed. However someone like Aristide who never had anything at all, who never knew how good it feels to have so much money and power, who ethically has nothing to give to society, when he finally gets to the top, his head spins, he becomes lost in his own arrogance and takes it all for himself. He neglects his past, he forgets his promises, and he eventually falls on his quest in the presence of all, and dies remorselessly, with no pity from anyone, even from those who once believed in him.

The mentality of man does not allow someone to love his enemy, it doesn't teach a man to show good faith toward someone else who has brought harm to him, although he may have found forgiveness within his heart. A man should walk and act and behave in manners of good standing and good character, so that if or when adversities ever strike, he could have someone to stand by him or speak for him. As long as the earth remains intact, there will always be tomorrow. One day the sun will be obstructed by the clouds, there will be rain and the umbrella will come in handy, therefore do not abuse the umbrella though it may seem insignificant on sunny days.

My fury has been generated from what I know, what I've heard and what I've personally experienced. There are families in Haiti who wake up in the morning, worn out through a long night cogitating on what they are going to feed their children.

Day after day they cope with the same excruciating moment in their life, thinking about how they are going to take care of themselves and their family. Factors like that can never be justified. That is certainly not the type of life any nation should have to live, or any parent would want to face, or any child deserves to know. Therefore how much less do I want to continually see my people and the children of my homeland living an daily life in such conditions!

What a people need to survive anywhere on this planet are the natural basic essential elements like foods and water, and clothes. However civilization has taken us many steps further, and we have been forced to seek knowledge in order to help and protect ourselves from each other. I believe if we kept the natural lifestyle we were created to follow as in the primitive world, things would have been less complex, life would have been easier, and we would have been happier people raising happier families. But because of what we have done to our environment, and what we have created that effect our lives in many negative ways, we have found ourselves in a position where we need to seek and research and contrive ways to counter our mishaps, and protect ourselves from the enemies that we have created, that are prone to destroy us. This is when we also gather in conclave and come up with laws and regulations to be voted on and constituted, which everyone in a particular society is to abide by.

Every human being is born with some natural deific rights, rights that cannot be granted by other human beings, but are given to every man by the Creator, to live and function on this planet as who we are, as God intended it to be. These rights have for attributes the right to be free, the right to be at peace, the right to exploit our talents and skills to improve the way we live, to survive in the most comfortable way possible, until we inhale our last breath.

Our societies have forced us into challenging one another through education, so we can secure our future in a social world that seems to be getting more exigent as we walk into new decades and millenniums. Everything in life requires knowledge and experiences, or natural instincts and discernment for those who believe in natural or supernatural powers, or simply luck for those atheists who believe they are controlled by forces in the firmament and around them, forces that are out of their control and understanding.

Having something is one thing, but managing it is another. Inviting the poor and the homeless into the presidential palace for a feast like Aristide once did is one thing, but providing them with resources to have foods and water to consume on a daily basis with their family, now there lies the challenge, and facing that challenge and overcoming it is the big difference.

A True Leader

What does it mean to be a leader?

A leader is someone who directs someone else, or a multitude of people, or a flock of animals onto a specific path. In every institution, any government, or any group small or large, there must be a leader. Without a leader everyone would be going on different directions, there would be no discipline. One would pull here while another pulls there, there would be nothing but chaos and havoc, and no goals would be achieved, no destination would be attained. But in the case of governing a country, a leader is not actually leading a group to a set destination, but in fact leading a nation toward a better way of life, to help them attain successful endeavors, and to provide them with security, allowing them to be and feel independent under governmental policies and constitutional laws and regulations. A leader in such position is not to pursue his or her objectives alone; therefore there must be acolytes as helping hands in the movements to advance the country to success, and fulfillment of great ambitions for the people. Know and remember that everyone has a place in society. We can't place a stethoscope in the hands of a farmer; he wouldn't know what to do with it. We can't put a basketball player on a soccer field, nor can we dress up an auto mechanic in expensive suits and have him fight our cases in court, those would definitely be lost cases. Likewise, we cannot place illiterate, uneducated, arrogant men in public offices. Again under the Lavalas era I've seen and heard it all. I have witnessed government representatives on television, degrading the Haitian community by their appearances, baffling people by their inarticulate and informal speeches, getting sidetracked and losing their topics as they prattle on the television screen. Those people are the ones Aristide had associated himself with. We find them in the mayoral offices, in the senate committee, and in most of the public institutions under the Lavalas emblem.

A leader is a role model, someone whose deeds and character acquire him respect and reverence from everyone and anyone regardless of age, gender, religion, educational background or social status. A leader is someone who is caring, full of compassion and respect for other human beings and their rights. A leader is not a terminology to be taking for granted, to fill someone with arrogance, to feel important in the mind of others, but someone who is convoked and elected to perform the duties of a benevolent, a protagonist, a father to a nation, prolonged by countless responsibilities. Surely not anyone is fit to be a leader. A true leader would rather stay hungry while he distributes his food to his flock. A true leader would put himself in harms way to save those who believe and trust in him, even if it means to sacrifice everything he has. A leader is a provider, a doctor, a protector, a teacher, a guide, someone who is supportive, trustworthy, honest, patient, comprehensive, loving and caring. A leader is full of strength, when his people and his disciples succumb, he always finds a way to encourage them even when he sees no hope, even when he too is discouraged and afflicted.

A leader is someone who understands the suffering of others, who is always in the position to listen to the supplications of his fellow men, while he sets his own problems aside, as he tries with all his might to resolve their problems before his.

No one expects another human being to be impeccable at everything, not a father, not a mother, not a friend, not a pastor, and certainly not a politician, although each of those figures is a leader as well on his or her term, on their own turf, they all need to try to fulfill their obligations to the best of their abilities. A president is someone who has been scrutinized and elected by the people to lead them and their country toward better days of peace, of happiness and prosperity. A president takes an oath to be an executioner of the legislative and judicial provisions of the nation, someone who will meet the necessities of his beloved people. We don't expect a leader to be capable of solving every problem that is presented to him, it is impossible to satisfy everyone's needs, but what really count sometimes is just the will to listen and put the efforts out to do something about it, as little as it may be, to give some type of satisfaction to the hope seeker. No president will ever be able to change the situation in which Haiti has been for the past decades. One term or even two terms of four years will certainly not be sufficient to bring Haiti and its people where they should be. It will take decades to accommodate at least a quarter of the Haitian population with the modern lifestyle found in the most developed countries around the globe, and about half a century with innumerable workmanship to introduce the whole population to true modernization. Nevertheless, I will not accept that declaration from any president, past, present or future, or any leader, as an excuse for failure to do their part during their reign in Haiti. For the past two hundred years since we have been independent, if every leader who had entered the National Palace had taken their vows in consideration toward Haiti, and not their arrogant desires, if they have done at least five percent of what they were supposed to do, then by now Haiti would have been the true Pearle of the Caribbean. If every leader had taken initiative to pave at least one mile of the rough roads in Haiti, then by now at least the capital of the country, Port-au-prince, would have been completely asphalted.

A leader sometimes needs to set aside his pen and paper, quit seeking for metaphorical terminologies to mislead the nation, and step out of the presidential territories, and head down to the slums, down to cite soleil, to the suburbs, pay a visit to those in the provinces, toward the extremity of the island, and see the various conditions in which the people are living with their family in shanties, in deserted environments. Speaking several languages, publishing many books, being famous for being the first president ever in the history of Haiti to have been overthrown, went into exile and reinstated to power, that is something relevant to one's popularity, something one should have gratitude for, however when it comes to a nation being under your control and security, the basic concern is not your personal endeavors and achievements. In the condition we are now, it should no longer be all about politics. This is the moment we analyze ourselves, examine our heart and spirit, to prove that we do have heart of flesh and not of stone, to prove that we are indeed a people of liberty, who believe in equality, who can survive in fraternity.

No one should ever assume that he or she will be loved and appreciated by everyone, it's merely impossible no matter what someone does in the eyes of man. There will be haters, there will be criticism. Some will notice your positive deeds and congratulate you, some will become friends and some will become enemies, but the bottom line is being peaceful with your spirit, judging that every step taken and every word spoken and everything procuring is justified. Jesus Christ as God reincarnated in human flesh in order to carry out a specific mission, came and lived among us. He taught peace, brotherhood and love, but though he came not to condemn the world despite the faulty deeds and impure actions of men, but to give life both physically and spiritually, yet they had the audacity and the courage to treat Him in the most humiliating, and excruciating manner that no man could ever bear to endure. He did absolutely nothing wrong to anyone and yet they hated Him with such passion to the point of crucifying Him in such inhumane way. Transformed by dehydration, from His final words "All is fulfilled" to His last breath He was faultless. If humans found the hatred within to commit murder to the perfect Man Jesus Christ, imagine how much worse they would treat another human being who is like themselves imperfect in every natural way. Imagine how much pain they can inflict onto another human being. We need each other like the body needs oxygen to subsist. It is our duty to love and care for one another. What would the world be without me and you? How would Adam survive if all he had were simply the different creatures that were in no shape or form related to him? No one can experience being alone anywhere and survive, not in a country, and certainly not in the world, just thinking about it is horrifying. Only if that was possible to experience, then we would have realized how indispensable we are to one another, and maybe we would treat and care for one another differently, with more understanding, with more compassion and mutual love.

Aristide had anticipated on legalizing the practice of voodoo as an official sect in Haiti. This new promotion would have granted the voodoo priests the rights to conduct wedding ceremonies, burials, witchcrafts, and other sacred ceremonies that only ordained ministers should be permitted to perform. A license which would give consent to a broader opportunity for voodoo priests to practice their wickedness with the supports and protection of the government. In some countries if someone does practice voodoo or witchcrafts, it's usually secretive, and recidivists would be expelled far away from civilization or even be put to death. Now in a country that has been bound by satanic forces for centuries, where people have been decimated by diseases and other natural catastrophic events, a former Catholic priest who has become president has found nothing better to offer to a vulnerable nation and its distressful country, but a license to practice voodoo. A tradition that would give roots to immorality, abomination, and illiteracy, which would certainly fan up the painful situations of the people, leading them deeper into deplorable predicaments. Aristide is a reprobate who should be stopped before he gets further in his quest to cede our land to the devil.

Sociology and Religions

I perceive religion as a theory, a belief, a lifestyle, and most of all a practice. Religions are juxtaposed to laws of civilizations, and it is nothing mysterious to say that laws of humanity and civilization are facsimiles to those of religions. Most religions preach against deceit, although it may seem trivial compared to rape or murder and other type of violence, or sins committed in a civilized nation. In the courtroom, before anyone takes the stand, he or she has to swear to tell the truth and nothing but the truth, as the right hand is erected and the left placing on the Bible. Is that more significant than proving the accused guilty of a crime? Certainly yes. Because if the truth is not told, someone may walk out exonerated though he or she is the one who actually committed the crime. Or someone may be incarcerated for a crime that he or she did not commit.

Religions teach people to live according to a standard that is justifiable, ethical, to protect, to respect, and to embrace the values of humanity. Different religion teaches different theories. To me, religion stands side by side with sociology. A theory is a belief, a belief is a standard, and a standard is a daily lifestyle to someone who is faithful and loyal to his religion. Based on an individual's belief, it's easy for others to characterize him and presume his lifestyle. It is easier to presume what that person is capable of doing, according to what he's been taught, even by whom he's been taught, according to his principles. Therefore legalizing the practice of voodoo in Haiti would further stipulate on the stereotype I've been hearing for years, that voodoo is originated from Haiti, which is in fact not a reputation to be proud of. This movement would have been a cataclysm, which would have plunged the country into abyss. The Haitian people need to open their eyes to see the wickedness within that man, by which he's been animated to deceive and decimate the population. Haiti is no one's personal estate to do whatever anybody pleases to do with it. Haiti is an independent country, where people should be involved in every decision that is being taken on their behalf and their country. From the very first time I heard his name and saw his face, I had a prescience that Aristide was not a sincere person, and no matter what he does or says there are some hearts he just can never deceive, and some men and women he can never convince. I can see all through him. He is a snake, a snare to all his followers, even to himself and he doesn't even know it. It's just a matter of time before his last day comes. He can't manage the country or the well being of the Haitian people. He does not know the value of such a great nation. Let us stand and mobilize to shovel away the dust of poverty, to eradicate the spirit of obscurity, to fight the forces of evil, and to combat misanthropes from our land of honor. We need to be vigilant in choosing our leaders. Our land is in distress, our trees are extirpated, our livestock is being decimated, our birds dissipating, our children dying of malnutrition, our students and journalists are being abducted. What type of plagues are we dealing with, what has pervaded our land? Rise up people; rise up with strength and power to fight the battle of the century before we see our generations exterminated and our country back in bondage. That's exactly what some people are waiting to witness, and they would do whatever it takes to make it a reality. For they believe in jealousy, they indulge in destruction as they push others to crumble.

The first time I sat down and cogitate on life, I realized that it the most essential, and the greatest gift a human being could ever possess, and it could be as easy or difficult as mysterious as it is. I finally had the innate evolution that has animated me toward a different direction, and that evolution led me to be more extroverted around other people, to care more about human interests and their well being. I concluded to believe that a heart is not too adamant to change for the better, to be saturated with love and sincerity, with compassion, with mutual comprehension, with sympathy and forgiveness toward co-habitants of Earth, and co-citizens of our Heavenly Father's estates. If everyone would be blessed with the spirit of discernment, to see life in its plenitude as special and essential as it is, to give it the importance it deserves, then life would be the best asset a living being would ever possess, and the world with every single soul respectively would be a much wonderful place we all would regret to leave behind.

CONTENTS

www.ingramcontent.com/pod-product-compliance
Lightning Source LLC
Chambersburg PA
CBHW020240290526
45784CB00003B/1058